VB6 SOURCE CODE: WINMGMTS EXECNOTIFICATIONQUERY ASYNC

__InstanceOperationEvent

Richard Edwards

INTRODUCTION

This book is constructed in a rather unique way.

Most books, by nature, are written by subject experts who are very good at what they do. Very few are written by real programmers.

Programmers are the druids of computer programming. They tend to be soft spoken and easy going. Very focused and not wandering far from the computer keyboard.

I am neither one.

I am a writer who has been a programmer, developer and a solution expert for over the past 30 years. And as such, I am wanting to share my work with you in a rather unique way.

The book was written around the work contained in one module that from top to bottom comes out to 1850 lines of tested and reusable code. It was written in roughly 2 hours and it will take me the better part of a day for me to explain what each routine does and how you can make the routine more robust.

I can't do all of the work for you. Your own personal touch can go a long- ways.

There are also 10 pages of code which will help you create a physical overview of all namespaces and classes that is currently on your dev box. Beyond that, the rest of the work in this book is designed to be called by a form with the intent to produce reusable code.

Unfortunately, many of the routines in this book are also dedicated in that they must be used by the Win32_Process. But you can and should be able to see where changing the word Process to Bios, ComputerSystem, Product, or over 700 other names can easily turn the routines into something else entirely different.

WHAT WMI NAMESPACES AND CLASSES ARE ON YOUR MACHINE?

Someone once said, "It is what you don't know that can kill you," Well, they might not have said it exactly that way, but you get the idea.

How can you use something that exists on your machine, but you don't know it?

Back in 2002, I created something called the WMI Explorer. Microsoft came out with their version in May of 2003. Neither one of us cared, It pretty much fell flat on its face.

The biggest difference between the two is my class groupings was based on the way the classes were presented. In-other-words, I there was no underscore, the category was the classname. If there was an underscore at the beginning of the classname, it was a superclass. It there was an underscore in the middle of the classname, the letters before the underscore became its category.

I thought it was a pretty good idea at the time.

Apparently, no one else did. Fact is, the concept was never used by anyone else and WMI Explorer that other people began to "create" used the Microsoft template and never did consider a more granular approach.

I also think the other reason why the WMI Explorer didn't become popular was because of the lack of documentation beyond the most common root: root\cimv2. And back in 2003 time, there were less than a few hundred of them.

But today is a completely different ballpark. Today there are literally hundreds of classes under root\cimv2 alone.

Would you like your own personal copy?

The following scripts that I've been using since 2002, will make that happen for you. Just create a folder on your desktop, then copy and paste the three scripts into that directory and start with namespaces.vbs and end with classes.vbs.

NAMESPACES.VBS

```
Dim fso
Dim l
Dim s


EnumNamespaces("root")

Sub EnumNamespaces(ByVal nspace)

Set ws = CreateObject("Wscript.Shell")
Set fso = CreateObject("Scripting.FilesystemObject")

If fso.folderExists(ws.currentDirectory & "\" & nspace) = false then
fso.CreateFolder(ws.currentDirectory & "\" & nspace)
End If

On error Resume Next

Set        objs        =        GetObject("Winmgmts:\\.\" &
nspace).InstancesOf("__Namespace", &H20000)

If err.Number <> 0 Then
err.Clear
Exit Sub
End If

For each obj in objs
```

```
    EnumNamespaces(nspace & "\" & obj.Name)
    Next

    End Sub
```

Categories.VBS

```
    Dim fso
    Dim l
    Dim s

    Set ws = CreateObject("Wscript.Shell")
    Set fso = CreateObject("Scripting.FilesystemObject")

    EnumNamespaces("root")


    Sub EnumNamespaces(ByVal nspace)

    EnumCategories(nspace)

    If fso.folderExists(ws.currentDirectory & "\" & nspace) = false then
    fso.CreateFolder(ws.currentDirectory & "\" & nspace)
    End If

    On error Resume Next

    Set        objs        =        GetObject("Winmgmts:\\.\"        &
    nspace).InstancesOf("___Namespace", &H20000)

    If err.Number <> 0 Then
    err.Clear
    Exit Sub
```

```
End If

For each obj in objs

EnumNamespaces(nspace & "\" & obj.Name)

Next

End Sub

Sub EnumCategories(ByVal nspace)

Set ws = CreateObject("Wscript.Shell")
Set fso = CreateObject("Scripting.FilesystemObject")

Set objs = GetObject("Winmgmts:\\.\" & nspace).SubClassesOf("", &H20000)
For each obj in objs

pos = instr(obj.Path_.class, "_")

if pos = 0 then
If fso.folderExists(ws.currentDirectory & "\" & nspace & "\" & obj.Path_.Class)
= false then
fso.CreateFolder(ws.currentDirectory & "\" & nspace & "\" & obj.Path_.Class)
End If
else
if pos = 1 then
If fso.folderExists(ws.currentDirectory & "\" & nspace & "\SuperClasses") =
false then
fso.CreateFolder(ws.currentDirectory & "\" & nspace & "\SuperClasses")
End If
else
```

```
        If    fso.folderExists(ws.currentDirectory   &   "\"   &   nspace   &   "\"   &
Mid(obj.Path_.Class, 1, pos-1)) = false then
        fso.CreateFolder(ws.currentDirectory      &      "\"     &     nspace     &     "\"     &
Mid(obj.Path_.Class, 1, pos-1))
        End If
        End If
        End If

        Next

        End Sub
```

Classes.VBS

```
        Dim fso
        Dim l
        Dim s

        EnumNamespaces("root")

        Sub EnumNamespaces(ByVal nspace)

        EnumClasses(nspace)

        Set ws = CreateObject("Wscript.Shell")
        Set fso = CreateObject("Scripting.FilesystemObject")

        If fso.folderExists(ws.currentDirectory & "\" & nspace) = false then
        fso.CreateFolder(ws.currentDirectory & "\" & nspace)
        End If

        On error Resume Next
```

```vbscript
    Set        objs        =         GetObject("Winmgmts:\\.\"        &
nspace).InstancesOf("___Namespace", &H20000)

    If err.Number <> 0 Then
    err.Clear
    Exit Sub
    End If

    For each obj in objs

    EnumNamespaces(nspace & "\" & obj.Name)

    Next

    End Sub

    Sub EnumClasses(ByVal nspace)

    Set ws = CreateObject("Wscript.Shell")
    Set fso = CreateObject("Scripting.FilesystemObject")

    Set objs = GetObject("Winmgmts:\\.\" & nspace).SubClassesOf("", &H20000)
    For each obj in objs

    pos = instr(obj.Path_.class, "_")

    if pos = 0 then
    call   CreateXMLFile(ws.CurrentDirectory   &   "\"   &   nspace   &   "\"   &
obj.Path_.Class, nspace, obj.Path_.Class)
    else
    if pos = 1 then
```

```vbscript
call CreateXMlFile(ws.CurrentDirectory & "\" & nspace & "\Superclasses",
nspace, obj.Path_.Class)
    else
    call CreateXMLFile(ws.CurrentDirectory & "\" & nspace & "\" &
Mid(obj.Path_.Class, 1, pos-1), nspace, obj.Path_.Class)
    End If
    End If

    Next

    End Sub

    Sub CreateXMLFile(ByVal Path, ByVal nspace, ByVal ClassName)



    Set fso = CreateObject("Scripting.FileSystemObject")
    Dim shorty
    On error Resume Next
    shorty = fso.GetFolder(Path).ShortPath
    If err.Number <> 0 then
    err.Clear
    Exit Sub
    End IF



    set obj = GetObject("Winmgmts:\\.\" & nspace).Get(classname)

    Set txtstream = fso.OpenTextFile(Shorty & "\" & Classname & ".xml", 2, true, -
2)
    txtstream.WriteLine("<data>")
    txtstream.WriteLine(" <NamespaceInformation>")
    txtstream.WriteLine("  <namespace>" & nspace & "</namespace>")
```

```
txtstream.WriteLine("    <classname>" & classname & "</classname>")
txtstream.WriteLine(" </NamespaceInformation>")
txtstream.WriteLine(" <properties>")

for each prop in obj.Properties_
txtstream.WriteLine("        <property Name = """ & prop.Name & """
IsArray=""" & prop.IsArray & """ DataType = """ &
prop.Qualifiers_("CIMType").Value & """/>")
Next
txtstream.WriteLine(" </properties>")
txtstream.WriteLine("</data>")
txtstream.close

End sub
```

As shown below, once these routines are done, you should be able to go to the folder, based on what I've told you about the Namespace\category\classes

Name	Date modified	Type
Win32_1394Controller	6/5/2018 6:41 PM	XML File
Win32_1394ControllerDevice	6/5/2018 6:41 PM	XML File
Win32_Account	6/5/2018 6:41 PM	XML File
Win32_AccountSID	6/5/2018 6:41 PM	XML File
Win32_ACE	6/5/2018 6:41 PM	XML File
Win32_ActionCheck	6/5/2018 6:42 PM	XML File
Win32_ActiveRoute	6/5/2018 6:41 PM	XML File
Win32_AllocatedResource	6/5/2018 6:41 PM	XML File
Win32_ApplicationCommandLine	6/5/2018 6:41 PM	XML File
Win32_ApplicationService	6/5/2018 6:41 PM	XML File
Win32_AssociatedProcessorMemory	6/5/2018 6:41 PM	XML File
Win32_AutochkSetting	6/5/2018 6:41 PM	XML File
Win32_BaseBoard	6/5/2018 6:41 PM	XML File
Win32_BaseService	6/5/2018 6:41 PM	XML File
Win32_Battery	6/5/2018 6:41 PM	XML File
Win32_Binary	6/5/2018 6:41 PM	XML File
Win32_BindImageAction	6/5/2018 6:41 PM	XML File
Win32_BIOS	6/5/2018 6:41 PM	XML File
Win32_BootConfiguration	6/5/2018 6:41 PM	XML File
Win32_Bus	6/5/2018 6:41 PM	XML File
Win32_CacheMemory	6/5/2018 6:41 PM	XML File
Win32_CDROMDrive	6/5/2018 6:41 PM	XML File
Win32_CheckCheck	6/5/2018 6:42 PM	XML File
Win32_CIMLogicalDeviceCIMDataFile	6/5/2018 6:41 PM	XML File
Win32_ClassicCOMApplicationClasses	6/5/2018 6:41 PM	XML File

686 items

And If you open one of these up:

```xml
- <data>
  - <NamespaceInformation>
      <namespace>root\CIMV2</namespace>
      <classname>Win32_BIOS</classname>
    </NamespaceInformation>
  - <properties>
      <property Name="BiosCharacteristics" IsArray="True" DataType="uint16"/>
      <property Name="BIOSVersion" IsArray="True" DataType="string"/>
      <property Name="BuildNumber" IsArray="False" DataType="string"/>
      <property Name="Caption" IsArray="False" DataType="string"/>
      <property Name="CodeSet" IsArray="False" DataType="string"/>
      <property Name="CurrentLanguage" IsArray="False" DataType="string"/>
      <property Name="Description" IsArray="False" DataType="string"/>
      <property Name="IdentificationCode" IsArray="False" DataType="string"/>
      <property Name="InstallableLanguages" IsArray="False" DataType="uint16"/>
      <property Name="InstallDate" IsArray="False" DataType="datetime"/>
      <property Name="LanguageEdition" IsArray="False" DataType="string"/>
      <property Name="ListOfLanguages" IsArray="True" DataType="string"/>
      <property Name="Manufacturer" IsArray="False" DataType="string"/>
      <property Name="Name" IsArray="False" DataType="string"/>
      <property Name="OtherTargetOS" IsArray="False" DataType="string"/>
      <property Name="PrimaryBIOS" IsArray="False" DataType="boolean"/>
      <property Name="ReleaseDate" IsArray="False" DataType="datetime"/>
      <property Name="SerialNumber" IsArray="False" DataType="string"/>
      <property Name="SMBIOSBIOSVersion" IsArray="False" DataType="string"/>
      <property Name="SMBIOSMajorVersion" IsArray="False" DataType="uint16"/>
      <property Name="SMBIOSMinorVersion" IsArray="False" DataType="uint16"/>
      <property Name="SMBIOSPresent" IsArray="False" DataType="boolean"/>
      <property Name="SoftwareElementID" IsArray="False" DataType="string"/>
      <property Name="SoftwareElementState" IsArray="False" DataType="uint16"/>
      <property Name="Status" IsArray="False" DataType="string"/>
      <property Name="TargetOperatingSystem" IsArray="False" DataType="uint16"/>
      <property Name="Version" IsArray="False" DataType="string"/>
    </properties>
  </data>
```

DECLARING VARIABLES

Below is a list of variables declared for coding continuity.

Dim svc As SWbemServices

Dim es As SWbemEventSource

Dim ti As SWbemObject

Dim obj As SWbemObject

Dim prop As SWbemProperty

Dim ws As Object

Dim Value As String

Dim fso As Scripting.FileSystemObject

Dim txtstream As Scripting.TextStream

Dim Names As Scripting.Dictionary

Dim Rows As Scripting.Dictionary

Dim x As Long

Dim y As Long

Dim v As Long

THE INITIALIZATION CODE

```
Dim WithEvents sink As SWbemSink


Private      Sub      sink_OnObjectReady(ByVal      objWbemObject      As
WbemScripting.ISWbemObject,      ByVal      objWbemAsyncContext      As
WbemScripting.ISWbemNamedValueSet)

  If y = 5 Then
    sink.Cancel
    v = 1
    Exit Sub
  End If


  Set obj = objWbemObject.Properties_.Item("TargetInstance").Value
  Set cols = New Scripting.Dictionary
  For Each prop In objWbemObject.Properties_

    If y = 0 Then
      Call Names.Add(x, prop.Name)
    End If

    Call cols.Add(x, GetValue(prop.Name, objWbemObject))
    x = x + 1

  Next

  x = 0
  Call Rows.Add(y, cols)
```

```vb
    y = y + 1

End Sub


Private Sub Form_Load()

x = 0
y = 0
v = 0


    Set Names = New Scripting.Dictionary
    Set Rows = New Scripting.Dictionary

    Set svc = GetObject("winmgmts:\\.\root\cimv2")
    svc.Security_.AuthenticationLevel = wbemAuthenticationLevelPktPrivacy
    svc.Security_.ImpersonationLevel = wbemImpersonationLevelImpersonate

    Set sink = New WbemScripting.SWbemSink
    Call      svc.ExecNotificationQueryAsync(sink,      "Select      *      from
___InstanceOperationEvent within 1 where TargetInstance ISA 'Win32_Process'")


    Do While v = 0
        DoEvents
    Loop


    End Sub
```

THE GETVALUE FUNCTION

Unlike VB.Net, VBScript uses a different syntax when it comes to initialization of variables and string parsing. The GetValue function used in this book looks like this:

```
Public Function GetValue(ByVal Name, ByVal obj)

    Dim PName
    Dim tempstr
    Dim pos

    PName = Chr(9) + Name + " = "
    tempstr = obj.GetObjectText_
    pos = InStr(tempstr, PName)

    If pos > 0 Then

        pos = pos + Len(PName)
        tempstr = Mid(tempstr, pos, Len(tempstr))
        pos = InStr(tempstr, ";")
        tempstr = Mid(tempstr, 1, pos – 1)
        tempstr = Replace(tempstr, Chr(34), "")
        tempstr = Replace(tempstr, "}", "")
        tempstr = Replace(tempstr, "{", "")
        tempstr = Trim(tempstr)
        If Len(tempstr) > 14 Then

            If obj.Properties_.Item(Name).CIMType = 101 Then
```

```
        Dim tstr
        tstr = Mid(tempstr, 5, 2)
        tstr = tstr + "/"
        tstr = tstr + Mid(tempstr, 7, 2)
        tstr = tstr + "/"
        tstr = tstr + Mid(tempstr, 1, 4)
        tstr = tstr + " "
        tstr = tstr + Mid(tempstr, 9, 2)
        tstr = tstr + ":"
        tstr = tstr + Mid(tempstr, 11, 2)
        tstr = tstr + ":"
        tstr = tstr + Mid(tempstr, 13, 2)
        tempstr = tstr

    End If
  End If

  GetValue = tempstr

Else

  GetValue = ""

End If

End Function
```

WHAT THE COMPLETED SCRIPT WOULD LOOK LIKE

Here's what the completed script would look like:

```
Dim l As SWbemLocator
Dim svc As SWbemServices
Dim ob As SWbemObject
Dim objs As SWbemObjectSet
Dim obj As SWbemObject
Dim prop As SWbemProperty

Dim Value As String

Dim Orientation As String

Dim ws As Object
Dim fso As Scripting.FileSystemObject
Dim txtstream As Scripting.TextStream
Dim Names As Scripting.Dictionary
Dim Rows As Scripting.Dictionary

Dim x As Long
Dim y As Long

Dim WithEvents sink As SWbemSink
```

```vb
Private Sub sink_OnObjectReady(ByVal objWbemObject As
WbemScripting.ISWbemObject, ByVal objWbemAsyncContext As
WbemScripting.ISWbemNamedValueSet)

    If y = 5 Then
        sink.Cancel
        v = 1
        Exit Sub
    End If


    Set obj = objWbemObject.Properties_.Item("TargetInstance").Value
    Set cols = New Scripting.Dictionary
    For Each prop In objWbemObject.Properties_

        If y = 0 Then
            Call Names.Add(x, prop.Name)
        End If

        Call cols.Add(x, GetValue(prop.Name, objWbemObject))
        x = x + 1

    Next

    x = 0
    Call Rows.Add(y, cols)
    y = y + 1

End Sub


Private Sub Form_Load()
```

```vbscript
    x = 0
    y = 0
    v = 0


    Set Names = New Scripting.Dictionary
    Set Rows = New Scripting.Dictionary

    Set svc = GetObject("winmgmts:\\.\root\cimv2")
    svc.Security_.AuthenticationLevel = wbemAuthenticationLevelPktPrivacy
    svc.Security_.ImpersonationLevel = wbemImpersonationLevelImpersonate

    Set sink = New WbemScripting.SWbemSink
    Call        svc.ExecNotificationQueryAsync(sink,        "Select      *      from
___InstanceOperationEvent within 1 where TargetInstance ISA 'Win32_Process'")

    Do While v = 0
       DoEvents
    Loop

    Orientation = "Multi-Line Horizontal"
    Create_The_HTML_Code

  End Sub


  Public Sub Create_The_HTML_Code()

    Set ws = CreateObject("WScript.Shell")

    Set fso = CreateObject("Scripting.FileSystemObject")
    Set txtstream = fso.OpenTextFile(ws.CurrentDirectory +
"\\Win32_Process.html", 2, True, -2)
    txtstream.WriteLine ("<html xmlns=""http://www.w3.org/1999/xhtml"">")
    txtstream.WriteLine ("<head>")
    txtstream.WriteLine ("<head>")
```

```
txtstream.WriteLine ("<style type='text/css'>")
txtstream.WriteLine ("body")
txtstream.WriteLine ("{")
txtstream.WriteLine ("    PADDING-RIGHT: 0px;")
txtstream.WriteLine ("    PADDING-LEFT: 0px;")
txtstream.WriteLine ("    PADDING-BOTTOM: 0px;")
txtstream.WriteLine ("    MARGIN: 0px;")
txtstream.WriteLine ("    COLOR: #333;")
txtstream.WriteLine ("    PADDING-TOP: 0px;")
txtstream.WriteLine ("    FONT-FAMILY: verdana, arial, helvetica, sans-serif;")
txtstream.WriteLine ("}")
txtstream.WriteLine ("table")
txtstream.WriteLine ("{")
txtstream.WriteLine ("    BORDER-RIGHT: #999999 1px solid;")
txtstream.WriteLine ("    PADDING-RIGHT: 1px;")
txtstream.WriteLine ("    PADDING-LEFT: 1px;")
txtstream.WriteLine ("    PADDING-BOTTOM: 1px;")
txtstream.WriteLine ("    LINE-HEIGHT: 8px;")
txtstream.WriteLine ("    PADDING-TOP: 1px;")
txtstream.WriteLine ("    BORDER-BOTTOM: #999 1px solid;")
txtstream.WriteLine ("    BACKGROUND-COLOR: #eeeeee;")
txtstream.WriteLine ("    filter:progid:DXImageTransform.Microsoft.Shadow(color='silver', Direction=135, Strength=16)")
txtstream.WriteLine ("}")
txtstream.WriteLine ("th")
txtstream.WriteLine ("{")
txtstream.WriteLine ("    BORDER-RIGHT: #999999 3px solid;")
txtstream.WriteLine ("    PADDING-RIGHT: 6px;")
txtstream.WriteLine ("    PADDING-LEFT: 6px;")
txtstream.WriteLine ("    FONT-WEIGHT: Bold;")
txtstream.WriteLine ("    FONT-SIZE: 14px;")
txtstream.WriteLine ("    PADDING-BOTTOM: 6px;")
txtstream.WriteLine ("    COLOR: darkred;")
txtstream.WriteLine ("    LINE-HEIGHT: 14px;")
txtstream.WriteLine ("    PADDING-TOP: 6px;")
txtstream.WriteLine ("    BORDER-BOTTOM: #999 1px solid;")
txtstream.WriteLine ("    BACKGROUND-COLOR: #eeeeee;")
txtstream.WriteLine ("    FONT-FAMILY: font-family: Cambria, serif;")
```

```
txtstream.WriteLine ("    FONT-SIZE: 12px;")
txtstream.WriteLine ("    text-align: left;")
txtstream.WriteLine ("    white-Space: nowrap;")
txtstream.WriteLine ("}")
txtstream.WriteLine (".th")
txtstream.WriteLine ("{")
txtstream.WriteLine ("    BORDER-RIGHT: #999999 2px solid;")
txtstream.WriteLine ("    PADDING-RIGHT: 6px;")
txtstream.WriteLine ("    PADDING-LEFT: 6px;")
txtstream.WriteLine ("    FONT-WEIGHT: Bold;")
txtstream.WriteLine ("    PADDING-BOTTOM: 6px;")
txtstream.WriteLine ("    COLOR: black;")
txtstream.WriteLine ("    PADDING-TOP: 6px;")
txtstream.WriteLine ("    BORDER-BOTTOM: #999 2px solid;")
txtstream.WriteLine ("    BACKGROUND-COLOR: #eeeeee;")
txtstream.WriteLine ("    FONT-FAMILY: font-family: Cambria, serif;")
txtstream.WriteLine ("    FONT-SIZE: 10px;")
txtstream.WriteLine ("    text-align: right;")
txtstream.WriteLine ("    white-Space: nowrap;")
txtstream.WriteLine ("}")
txtstream.WriteLine ("td")
txtstream.WriteLine ("{")
txtstream.WriteLine ("    BORDER-RIGHT: #999999 3px solid;")
txtstream.WriteLine ("    PADDING-RIGHT: 6px;")
txtstream.WriteLine ("    PADDING-LEFT: 6px;")
txtstream.WriteLine ("    FONT-WEIGHT: Normal;")
txtstream.WriteLine ("    PADDING-BOTTOM: 6px;")
txtstream.WriteLine ("    COLOR: navy;")
txtstream.WriteLine ("    LINE-HEIGHT: 14px;")
txtstream.WriteLine ("    PADDING-TOP: 6px;")
txtstream.WriteLine ("    BORDER-BOTTOM: #999 1px solid;")
txtstream.WriteLine ("    BACKGROUND-COLOR: #eeeeee;")
txtstream.WriteLine ("    FONT-FAMILY: font-family: Cambria, serif;")
txtstream.WriteLine ("    FONT-SIZE: 12px;")
txtstream.WriteLine ("    text-align: left;")
txtstream.WriteLine ("    white-Space: nowrap;")
txtstream.WriteLine ("}")
txtstream.WriteLine ("div")
txtstream.WriteLine ("{")
txtstream.WriteLine ("    BORDER-RIGHT: #999999 3px solid;")
```

```
txtstream.WriteLine ("    PADDING-RIGHT: 6px;")
txtstream.WriteLine ("    PADDING-LEFT: 6px;")
txtstream.WriteLine ("    FONT-WEIGHT: Normal;")
txtstream.WriteLine ("    PADDING-BOTTOM: 6px;")
txtstream.WriteLine ("    COLOR: white;")
txtstream.WriteLine ("    PADDING-TOP: 6px;")
txtstream.WriteLine ("    BORDER-BOTTOM: #999 1px solid;")
txtstream.WriteLine ("    BACKGROUND-COLOR: navy;")
txtstream.WriteLine ("    FONT-FAMILY: font-family: Cambria, serif;")
txtstream.WriteLine ("    FONT-SIZE: 10px;")
txtstream.WriteLine ("    text-align: left;")
txtstream.WriteLine ("    white-Space: nowrap;")
txtstream.WriteLine ("}")
txtstream.WriteLine ("span")
txtstream.WriteLine ("{")
txtstream.WriteLine ("    BORDER-RIGHT: #999999 3px solid;")
txtstream.WriteLine ("    PADDING-RIGHT: 3px;")
txtstream.WriteLine ("    PADDING-LEFT: 3px;")
txtstream.WriteLine ("    FONT-WEIGHT: Normal;")
txtstream.WriteLine ("    PADDING-BOTTOM: 3px;")
txtstream.WriteLine ("    COLOR: white;")
txtstream.WriteLine ("    PADDING-TOP: 3px;")
txtstream.WriteLine ("    BORDER-BOTTOM: #999 1px solid;")
txtstream.WriteLine ("    BACKGROUND-COLOR: navy;")
txtstream.WriteLine ("    FONT-FAMILY: font-family: Cambria, serif;")
txtstream.WriteLine ("    FONT-SIZE: 10px;")
txtstream.WriteLine ("    text-align: left;")
txtstream.WriteLine ("    white-Space: nowrap;")
txtstream.WriteLine ("    display: inline-block;")
txtstream.WriteLine ("    width: 100%;")
txtstream.WriteLine ("}")
txtstream.WriteLine ("textarea")
txtstream.WriteLine ("{")
txtstream.WriteLine ("    BORDER-RIGHT: #999999 3px solid;")
txtstream.WriteLine ("    PADDING-RIGHT: 3px;")
txtstream.WriteLine ("    PADDING-LEFT: 3px;")
txtstream.WriteLine ("    FONT-WEIGHT: Normal;")
txtstream.WriteLine ("    PADDING-BOTTOM: 3px;")
txtstream.WriteLine ("    COLOR: white;")
txtstream.WriteLine ("    PADDING-TOP: 3px;")
```

```
txtstream.WriteLine ("    BORDER-BOTTOM: #999 1px solid;")
txtstream.WriteLine ("    BACKGROUND-COLOR: navy;")
txtstream.WriteLine ("    FONT-FAMILY: font-family: Cambria, serif;")
txtstream.WriteLine ("    FONT-SIZE: 10px;")
txtstream.WriteLine ("    text-align: left;")
txtstream.WriteLine ("    white-Space: nowrap;")
txtstream.WriteLine ("    width: 100%;")
txtstream.WriteLine ("}")
txtstream.WriteLine ("select")
txtstream.WriteLine ("{")
txtstream.WriteLine ("    BORDER-RIGHT: #999999 3px solid;")
txtstream.WriteLine ("    PADDING-RIGHT: 6px;")
txtstream.WriteLine ("    PADDING-LEFT: 6px;")
txtstream.WriteLine ("    FONT-WEIGHT: Normal;")
txtstream.WriteLine ("    PADDING-BOTTOM: 6px;")
txtstream.WriteLine ("    COLOR: white;")
txtstream.WriteLine ("    PADDING-TOP: 6px;")
txtstream.WriteLine ("    BORDER-BOTTOM: #999 1px solid;")
txtstream.WriteLine ("    BACKGROUND-COLOR: navy;")
txtstream.WriteLine ("    FONT-FAMILY: font-family: Cambria, serif;")
txtstream.WriteLine ("    FONT-SIZE: 10px;")
txtstream.WriteLine ("    text-align: left;")
txtstream.WriteLine ("    white-Space: nowrap;")
txtstream.WriteLine ("    width: 100%;")
txtstream.WriteLine ("}")
txtstream.WriteLine ("input")
txtstream.WriteLine ("{")
txtstream.WriteLine ("    BORDER-RIGHT: #999999 3px solid;")
txtstream.WriteLine ("    PADDING-RIGHT: 3px;")
txtstream.WriteLine ("    PADDING-LEFT: 3px;")
txtstream.WriteLine ("    FONT-WEIGHT: Bold;")
txtstream.WriteLine ("    PADDING-BOTTOM: 3px;")
txtstream.WriteLine ("    COLOR: white;")
txtstream.WriteLine ("    PADDING-TOP: 3px;")
txtstream.WriteLine ("    BORDER-BOTTOM: #999 1px solid;")
txtstream.WriteLine ("    BACKGROUND-COLOR: navy;")
txtstream.WriteLine ("    FONT-FAMILY: font-family: Cambria, serif;")
txtstream.WriteLine ("    FONT-SIZE: 12px;")
txtstream.WriteLine ("    text-align: left;")
txtstream.WriteLine ("    display: table-cell;")
```

```
txtstream.WriteLine ("    white-Space: nowrap;")
txtstream.WriteLine ("    width: 100%;")
txtstream.WriteLine ("}")
txtstream.WriteLine ("h1 {")
txtstream.WriteLine ("color: antiquewhite;")
txtstream.WriteLine ("text-shadow: 1px 1px 1px black;")
txtstream.WriteLine ("padding: 3px;")
txtstream.WriteLine ("text-align: center;")
txtstream.WriteLine ("box-shadow: inset 2px 2px 5px rgba(0,0,0,0.5), inset -
2px -2px 5px rgba(255,255,255,0.5)")
txtstream.WriteLine ("}")
txtstream.WriteLine ("</style>")
txtstream.WriteLine ("<title>Win32_Process</title>")
txtstream.WriteLine ("</head>")
txtstream.WriteLine ("<body>")
txtstream.WriteLine ("<table Border='1' cellpadding='1' cellspacing='1'>")

Select Case Orientation

    Case "Single-Line Horizontal"

        txtstream.WriteLine ("<tr>")
        For x = 0 To Names.Count - 1
           txtstream.WriteLine ("<th>" + Names.Item(x) + "</th>")
        Next
        txtstream.WriteLine ("</tr>")
        txtstream.WriteLine ("<tr>")
        For x = 0 To Names.Count - 1
           txtstream.WriteLine ("<td>" + Rows.Item(y)(x) + "</td>")
        Next
        txtstream.WriteLine ("</tr>")

    Case "Multi-Line Horizontal"

        txtstream.WriteLine ("<tr>")
        For x = 0 To Names.Count - 1
           txtstream.WriteLine ("<th>" + Names.Item(x) + "</th>")
        Next
        txtstream.WriteLine ("</tr>")
```

```
        For y = 0 To Rows.Count - 1
           txtstream.WriteLine ("<tr>")
           For x = 0 To Names.Count - 1
              txtstream.WriteLine ("<td>" + Rows.Item(y)(x) + "</td>")
           Next
           txtstream.WriteLine ("</tr>")
        Next


     Case "Single-Line Vertical"


        For x = 0 To Names.Count - 1
           txtstream.WriteLine ("<tr><th>" + Names.Item(x) + "</th><td>" +
Rows.Item(y)(x) + "</td></tr>")
        Next


     Case "Multi-Line Vertical"


        For x = 0 To Names.Count - 1
           txtstream.WriteLine ("<tr><th>" + Names.Item(x) + "</th>")
           For y = 0 To Row.Count - 1
              txtstream.WriteLine ("<td>" + Rows.Item(y)(x) + "</td>")
           Next
           txtstream.WriteLine ("</tr>")
        Next


     End Select


  txtstream.WriteLine ("</table>")
  txtstream.WriteLine ("</body>")
  txtstream.WriteLine ("</html>")
  txtstream.Close


End Sub


Public Function GetValue(ByVal Name, ByVal obj)


  Dim PName
  Dim tempstr
  Dim pos
```

```
PName = Chr(9) + Name + " = "
tempstr = obj.GetObjectText_
pos = InStr(tempstr, PName)

If pos > 0 Then

    pos = pos + Len(PName)
    tempstr = Mid(tempstr, pos, Len(tempstr))
    pos = InStr(tempstr, ";")
    tempstr = Mid(tempstr, 1, pos - 1)
    tempstr = Replace(tempstr, Chr(34), "")
    tempstr = Replace(tempstr, "}", "")
    tempstr = Replace(tempstr, "{", "")
    tempstr = Trim(tempstr)

    If Len(tempstr) > 14 Then

        If obj.Properties_.Item(Name).CIMType = 101 Then

            Dim tstr
            tstr = Mid(tempstr, 5, 2)
            tstr = tstr + "/"
            tstr = tstr + Mid(tempstr, 7, 2)
            tstr = tstr + "/"
            tstr = tstr + Mid(tempstr, 1, 4)
            tstr = tstr + " "
            tstr = tstr + Mid(tempstr, 9, 2)
            tstr = tstr + ":"
            tstr = tstr + Mid(tempstr, 11, 2)
            tstr = tstr + ":"
            tstr = tstr + Mid(tempstr, 13, 2)
            tempstr = tstr

        End If

    End If

    GetValue = tempstr

Else
```

    GetValue = ""

    End If

End Function

And that produces this in a much larger scale:

Caption	CommandLine	^
System Idle Process		
System		
smss.exe		
csrss.exe		
csrss.exe		
wininit.exe		
winlogon.exe	winlogon.exe	
services.exe		
lsass.exe	C:\\Windows\\system32\\lsass.exe	
svchost.exe	C:\\Windows\\system32\\svchost.exe -k DcomLaunch	
svchost.exe	C:\\Windows\\system32\\svchost.exe -k RPCSS	
dwm.exe	\dwm.exe\	
svchost.exe	C:\\Windows\\System32\\svchost.exe -k termsvcs	
svchost.exe	C:\\Windows\\System32\\svchost.exe -k LocalSystemNetworkRestricted	
svchost.exe	C:\\Windows\\System32\\svchost.exe -k LocalServiceNetworkRestricted	
svchost.exe	C:\\Windows\\system32\\svchost.exe -k LocalServiceNoNetwork	
svchost.exe	C:\\Windows\\system32\\svchost.exe -k LocalService	
NVDisplay.Container.exe	\C:\\Program Files\\NVIDIA Corporation\\Display.NvContainer\\NVDisplay.Container.exe\ -s NVDisplay.ContainerLocalSystem -f \C:\\ProgramData\\NVIDIA\\NVDisplay.Containe	
svchost.exe	C:\\Windows\\System32\\svchost.exe -k NetworkService	
WUDFHost.exe	\C:\\\Windows\\System32\\WUDFHost.exe\ -HostGUID:193a1820-d9ac-4997-8c55-be817523f6aa -IoEventPortName:HostProcess-fa210d42-7ee3-474b-9ab6-807cd2ecd8e8 -Sy	
svchost.exe	C:\\Windows\\system32\\svchost.exe -k netsvcs	
svchost.exe	C:\\Windows\\system32\\svchost.exe -k LocalServiceNetworkRestricted	
svchost.exe	C:\\Windows\\system32\\svchost.exe -k WlansvcGroup	
svchost.exe	C:\\Windows\\system32\\svchost.exe -k LocalServiceNetworkRestricted	
spoolsv.exe	C:\\Windows\\System32\\spoolsv.exe	
svchost.exe	C:\\Windows\\system32\\svchost.exe -k apphost	

Of course, there are a lot of other ways you can create your code. Below, are some generic ideas to whet your appetite.

CREATE THE ASP CODE

Inside this sub routine is the code to create an ASP Webpage. You simply pass in the collection generated by the Return_Management_Collection and specify its orientation.

```
Public Sub Create_ASP_Code()

    Set ws = CreateObject("WScript.Shell")
    Set fso = CreateObject("Scripting.FileSystemObject")
    Set    txtstream    =    fso.OpenTextFile(ws.CurrentDirectory    +
"\\Win32_Process.asp", 2, True, -2)
    txtstream.WriteLine                                    ("<html
xmlns=""http://www.w3.org/1999/xhtml"">")
    txtstream.WriteLine ("<head>")
    txtstream.WriteLine ("<head>")
    txtstream.WriteLine ("<style type='text/css'>")
    txtstream.WriteLine ("body")
    txtstream.WriteLine ("{")
    txtstream.WriteLine ("   PADDING-RIGHT: 0px;")
    txtstream.WriteLine ("   PADDING-LEFT: 0px;")
    txtstream.WriteLine ("   PADDING-BOTTOM: 0px;")
    txtstream.WriteLine ("   MARGIN: 0px;")
    txtstream.WriteLine ("   COLOR: #333;")
    txtstream.WriteLine ("   PADDING-TOP: 0px;")
    txtstream.WriteLine ("    FONT-FAMILY: verdana, arial, helvetica, sans-
serif;")
    txtstream.WriteLine ("}")
    txtstream.WriteLine ("table")
    txtstream.WriteLine ("{")
```

```
txtstream.WriteLine ("    BORDER-RIGHT: #999999 1px solid;")
txtstream.WriteLine ("    PADDING-RIGHT: 1px;")
txtstream.WriteLine ("    PADDING-LEFT: 1px;")
txtstream.WriteLine ("    PADDING-BOTTOM: 1px;")
txtstream.WriteLine ("    LINE-HEIGHT: 8px;")
txtstream.WriteLine ("    PADDING-TOP: 1px;")
txtstream.WriteLine ("    BORDER-BOTTOM: #999 1px solid;")
txtstream.WriteLine ("    BACKGROUND COLOR: #eeeeee;")
txtstream.WriteLine                                        ("
filter:progid:DXImageTransform.Microsoft.Shadow(color='silver',    Direction=135,
Strength=16)")
txtstream.WriteLine ("}")
txtstream.WriteLine ("th")
txtstream.WriteLine ("{")
txtstream.WriteLine ("    BORDER-RIGHT: #999999 3px solid;")
txtstream.WriteLine ("    PADDING-RIGHT: 6px;")
txtstream.WriteLine ("    PADDING-LEFT: 6px;")
txtstream.WriteLine ("    FONT-WEIGHT: Bold;")
txtstream.WriteLine ("    FONT-SIZE: 14px;")
txtstream.WriteLine ("    PADDING-BOTTOM: 6px;")
txtstream.WriteLine ("    COLOR: darkred;")
txtstream.WriteLine ("    LINE-HEIGHT: 14px;")
txtstream.WriteLine ("    PADDING-TOP: 6px;")
txtstream.WriteLine ("    BORDER-BOTTOM: #999 1px solid;")
txtstream.WriteLine ("    BACKGROUND-COLOR: #eeeeee;")
txtstream.WriteLine ("    FONT-FAMILY: font-family: Cambria, serif;")
txtstream.WriteLine ("    FONT-SIZE: 12px;")
txtstream.WriteLine ("    text-align: left;")
txtstream.WriteLine ("    white-Space: nowrap;")
txtstream.WriteLine ("}")
txtstream.WriteLine (".th")
txtstream.WriteLine ("{")
txtstream.WriteLine ("    BORDER-RIGHT: #999999 2px solid;")
```

```
txtstream.WriteLine ("    PADDING-RIGHT: 6px;")
txtstream.WriteLine ("    PADDING-LEFT: 6px;")
txtstream.WriteLine ("    FONT-WEIGHT: Bold;")
txtstream.WriteLine ("    PADDING-BOTTOM: 6px;")
txtstream.WriteLine ("    COLOR: black;")
txtstream.WriteLine ("    PADDING-TOP: 6px;")
txtstream.WriteLine ("    BORDER-BOTTOM: #999 2px solid;")
txtstream.WriteLine ("    BACKGROUND-COLOR: #eeeeee;")
txtstream.WriteLine ("    FONT-FAMILY: font-family: Cambria, serif;")
txtstream.WriteLine ("    FONT-SIZE: 10px;")
txtstream.WriteLine ("    text-align: right;")
txtstream.WriteLine ("    white-Space: nowrap;")
txtstream.WriteLine ("}")
txtstream.WriteLine ("td")
txtstream.WriteLine ("{")
txtstream.WriteLine ("    BORDER-RIGHT: #999999 3px solid;")
txtstream.WriteLine ("    PADDING-RIGHT: 6px;")
txtstream.WriteLine ("    PADDING-LEFT: 6px;")
txtstream.WriteLine ("    FONT-WEIGHT: Normal;")
txtstream.WriteLine ("    PADDING-BOTTOM: 6px;")
txtstream.WriteLine ("    COLOR: navy;")
txtstream.WriteLine ("    LINE-HEIGHT: 14px;")
txtstream.WriteLine ("    PADDING-TOP: 6px;")
txtstream.WriteLine ("    BORDER-BOTTOM: #999 1px solid;")
txtstream.WriteLine ("    BACKGROUND-COLOR: #eeeeee;")
txtstream.WriteLine ("    FONT-FAMILY: font-family: Cambria, serif;")
txtstream.WriteLine ("    FONT-SIZE: 12px;")
txtstream.WriteLine ("    text-align: left;")
txtstream.WriteLine ("    white-Space: nowrap;")
txtstream.WriteLine ("}")
txtstream.WriteLine ("div")
txtstream.WriteLine ("{")
txtstream.WriteLine ("    BORDER-RIGHT: #999999 3px solid;")
```

```
txtstream.WriteLine ("   PADDING-RIGHT: 6px;")
txtstream.WriteLine ("   PADDING-LEFT: 6px;")
txtstream.WriteLine ("   FONT-WEIGHT: Normal;")
txtstream.WriteLine ("   PADDING-BOTTOM: 6px;")
txtstream.WriteLine ("   COLOR: white;")
txtstream.WriteLine ("   PADDING-TOP: 6px;")
txtstream.WriteLine ("   BORDER-BOTTOM: #999 1px solid;")
txtstream.WriteLine ("   BACKGROUND-COLOR: navy;")
txtstream.WriteLine ("   FONT-FAMILY: font-family: Cambria, serif;")
txtstream.WriteLine ("   FONT-SIZE: 10px;")
txtstream.WriteLine ("   text-align: left;")
txtstream.WriteLine ("   white-Space: nowrap;")
txtstream.WriteLine ("}")
txtstream.WriteLine ("span")
txtstream.WriteLine ("{")
txtstream.WriteLine ("   BORDER-RIGHT: #999999 3px solid;")
txtstream.WriteLine ("   PADDING-RIGHT: 3px;")
txtstream.WriteLine ("   PADDING-LEFT: 3px;")
txtstream.WriteLine ("   FONT-WEIGHT: Normal;")
txtstream.WriteLine ("   PADDING-BOTTOM: 3px;")
txtstream.WriteLine ("   COLOR: white;")
txtstream.WriteLine ("   PADDING-TOP: 3px;")
txtstream.WriteLine ("   BORDER-BOTTOM: #999 1px solid;")
txtstream.WriteLine ("   BACKGROUND-COLOR: navy;")
txtstream.WriteLine ("   FONT-FAMILY: font-family: Cambria, serif;")
txtstream.WriteLine ("   FONT-SIZE: 10px;")
txtstream.WriteLine ("   text-align: left;")
txtstream.WriteLine ("   white-Space: nowrap;")
txtstream.WriteLine ("   display: inline-block;")
txtstream.WriteLine ("   width: 100%;")
txtstream.WriteLine ("}")
txtstream.WriteLine ("textarea")
txtstream.WriteLine ("{")
```

```
txtstream.WriteLine ("    BORDER-RIGHT: #999999 3px solid;")
txtstream.WriteLine ("    PADDING-RIGHT: 3px;")
txtstream.WriteLine ("    PADDING-LEFT: 3px;")
txtstream.WriteLine ("    FONT-WEIGHT: Normal;")
txtstream.WriteLine ("    PADDING-BOTTOM: 3px;")
txtstream.WriteLine ("    COLOR: white;")
txtstream.WriteLine ("    PADDING-TOP: 3px;")
txtstream.WriteLine ("    BORDER-BOTTOM: #999 1px solid;")
txtstream.WriteLine ("    BACKGROUND-COLOR: navy;")
txtstream.WriteLine ("    FONT-FAMILY: font-family: Cambria, serif;")
txtstream.WriteLine ("    FONT-SIZE: 10px;")
txtstream.WriteLine ("    text-align: left;")
txtstream.WriteLine ("    white-Space: nowrap;")
txtstream.WriteLine ("    width: 100%;")
txtstream.WriteLine ("}")
txtstream.WriteLine ("select")
txtstream.WriteLine ("{")
txtstream.WriteLine ("    BORDER-RIGHT: #999999 3px solid;")
txtstream.WriteLine ("    PADDING-RIGHT: 6px;")
txtstream.WriteLine ("    PADDING-LEFT: 6px;")
txtstream.WriteLine ("    FONT-WEIGHT: Normal;")
txtstream.WriteLine ("    PADDING-BOTTOM: 6px;")
txtstream.WriteLine ("    COLOR: white;")
txtstream.WriteLine ("    PADDING-TOP: 6px;")
txtstream.WriteLine ("    BORDER-BOTTOM: #999 1px solid;")
txtstream.WriteLine ("    BACKGROUND-COLOR: navy;")
txtstream.WriteLine ("    FONT-FAMILY: font-family: Cambria, serif;")
txtstream.WriteLine ("    FONT-SIZE: 10px;")
txtstream.WriteLine ("    text-align: left;")
txtstream.WriteLine ("    white-Space: nowrap;")
txtstream.WriteLine ("    width: 100%;")
txtstream.WriteLine ("}")
txtstream.WriteLine ("input")
```

```
txtstream.WriteLine ("{")
txtstream.WriteLine ("    BORDER-RIGHT: #999999 3px solid;")
txtstream.WriteLine ("    PADDING-RIGHT: 3px;")
txtstream.WriteLine ("    PADDING-LEFT: 3px;")
txtstream.WriteLine ("    FONT-WEIGHT: Bold;")
txtstream.WriteLine ("    PADDING-BOTTOM: 3px;")
txtstream.WriteLine ("    COLOR: white;")
txtstream.WriteLine ("    PADDING-TOP: 3px;")
txtstream.WriteLine ("    BORDER-BOTTOM: #999 1px solid;")
txtstream.WriteLine ("    BACKGROUND-COLOR: navy;")
txtstream.WriteLine ("    FONT-FAMILY: font-family: Cambria, serif;")
txtstream.WriteLine ("    FONT-SIZE: 12px;")
txtstream.WriteLine ("    text-align: left;")
txtstream.WriteLine ("    display: table-cell;")
txtstream.WriteLine ("    white-Space: nowrap;")
txtstream.WriteLine ("    width: 100%;")
txtstream.WriteLine ("}")
txtstream.WriteLine ("h1 {")
txtstream.WriteLine ("color: antiquewhite;")
txtstream.WriteLine ("text-shadow: 1px 1px 1px black;")
txtstream.WriteLine ("padding: 3px;")
txtstream.WriteLine ("text-align: center;")
txtstream.WriteLine ("box-shadow: inset 2px 2px 5px rgba(0,0,0,0.5),
inset -2px -2px 5px rgba(255,255,255,0.5)")
txtstream.WriteLine ("}")
txtstream.WriteLine ("</style>")
txtstream.WriteLine ("<title>Win32_Process</title>")
txtstream.WriteLine ("</head>")
txtstream.WriteLine ("<body>")
txtstream.WriteLine ("<%")
txtstream.WriteLine ("Response.Write(""<table Border='1' cellpadding='1'
cellspacing='1'>"" & vbcrlf)")
```

```vb
Select Case Orientation

    Case "Single-Line Horizontal"

            txtstream.WriteLine ("Response.Write(""<tr>"" & vbcrlf)")
            For x = 0 To Names.Count -1
                txtstream.WriteLine ("Response.Write(""<th>" + Names.Item(x) + "</th>"" & vbcrlf)")
            Next
            txtstream.WriteLine ("Response.Write(""</tr>"" & vbcrlf)")
            txtstream.WriteLine ("Response.Write(""<tr>"" & vbcrlf)")
            For x = 0 To Names.Count -1
                txtstream.WriteLine        ("Response.Write(""<td>"        + Rows.Item(y)(x) + "</td>"" & vbcrlf)")
            Next
            txtstream.WriteLine ("Response.Write(""</tr>"" & vbcrlf)")


    Case "Multi-Line Horizontal"

            txtstream.WriteLine ("Response.Write(""<tr>"" & vbcrlf)")
            For x = 0 To Names.Count -1
                txtstream.WriteLine ("Response.Write(""<th>" + Names.Item(x) + "</th>"" & vbcrlf)")
            Next
            txtstream.WriteLine ("Response.Write(""</tr>"" & vbcrlf)")
            For y = 0 To  Rows.Count -1
                txtstream.WriteLine ("Response.Write(""<tr>"" & vbcrlf)")
                For x = 0 To Names.Count -1
                    txtstream.WriteLine        ("Response.Write(""<td>"        + Rows.Item(y)(x) + "</td>"" & vbcrlf)")
                Next
                txtstream.WriteLine ("Response.Write(""</tr>"" & vbcrlf)")
            Next
```

```vb
        Case "Single-Line Vertical"

            For x = 0 To Names.Count -1
                txtstream.WriteLine        ("Response.Write(""<tr><th>"        +
Names.Item(x) + "</th><td>" + Rows.Item(y)(x) + "</td></tr>"" & vbcrlf)")
            Next

        Case "Multi-Line Vertical"

            For x = 0 To Names.Count -1
                txtstream.WriteLine        ("Response.Write(""<tr><th>"        +
Names.Item(x) + "</th>"" & vbcrlf)")
                For y = 0 To Row.Count-1
                    txtstream.WriteLine        ("Response.Write(""<td>"        +
Rows.Item(y)(x) + "</td>"" & vbcrlf)")
                Next
                txtstream.WriteLine ("Response.Write(""</tr>"" & vbcrlf)")
            Next

    End Select

    txtstream.WriteLine ("Response.Write(""</table>"" & vbcrlf)")
    txtstream.WriteLine ("%>")
    txtstream.WriteLine ("</body>")
    txtstream.WriteLine ("</html>")
    txtstream.Close

End                                                                          Sub
```

CREATE ASPX CODE

Inside this sub routine is the code to create an ASPX Webpage. You simply pass in the collection generated by the Return_Management_Collection and specify its orientation.

```
Public Sub Create_ASPX_Code()

    Set ws = CreateObject("WScript.Shell")
    Set fso = CreateObject("Scripting.FileSystemObject")
    Set      txtstream   =   fso.OpenTextFile(ws.CurrentDirectory   +
"\\Win32_Process.aspx", 2, True, -2)
    txtstream.WriteLine ("<!DOCTYPE html PUBLIC ""-//W3C//DTD XHTML
1.0      Transitional//EN"""         ""http://www.w3.org/TR/xhtml1/DTD/xhtml1-
transitional.dtd""">")
    txtstream.WriteLine ("")
    txtstream.WriteLine                                            ("<html
xmlns=""http://www.w3.org/1999/xhtml"">")
    txtstream.WriteLine ("<head>")
    txtstream.WriteLine ("<style type='text/css'>")
    txtstream.WriteLine ("body")
    txtstream.WriteLine ("{")
    txtstream.WriteLine ("   PADDING-RIGHT: 0px;")
    txtstream.WriteLine ("   PADDING-LEFT: 0px;")
    txtstream.WriteLine ("   PADDING-BOTTOM: 0px;")
    txtstream.WriteLine ("   MARGIN: 0px;")
    txtstream.WriteLine ("   COLOR: #333;")
    txtstream.WriteLine ("   PADDING-TOP: 0px;")
    txtstream.WriteLine ("    FONT-FAMILY: verdana, arial, helvetica, sans-
serif;")
```

```
txtstream.WriteLine ("}")
txtstream.WriteLine ("table")
txtstream.WriteLine ("{")
txtstream.WriteLine ("    BORDER-RIGHT: #999999 1px solid;")
txtstream.WriteLine ("    PADDING-RIGHT: 1px;")
txtstream.WriteLine ("    PADDING-LEFT: 1px;")
txtstream.WriteLine ("    PADDING-BOTTOM: 1px;")
txtstream.WriteLine ("    LINE-HEIGHT: 8px;")
txtstream.WriteLine ("    PADDING-TOP: 1px;")
txtstream.WriteLine ("    BORDER-BOTTOM: #999 1px solid;")
txtstream.WriteLine ("    BACKGROUND-COLOR: #eeeeee;")
txtstream.WriteLine                                    ("
filter:progid:DXImageTransform.Microsoft.Shadow(color='silver',    Direction=135,
Strength=16)")
txtstream.WriteLine ("}")
txtstream.WriteLine ("th")
txtstream.WriteLine ("{")
txtstream.WriteLine ("    BORDER-RIGHT: #999999 3px solid;")
txtstream.WriteLine ("    PADDING-RIGHT: 6px;")
txtstream.WriteLine ("    PADDING-LEFT: 6px;")
txtstream.WriteLine ("    FONT-WEIGHT: Bold;")
txtstream.WriteLine ("    FONT-SIZE: 14px;")
txtstream.WriteLine ("    PADDING-BOTTOM: 6px;")
txtstream.WriteLine ("    COLOR: darkred;")
txtstream.WriteLine ("    LINE-HEIGHT: 14px;")
txtstream.WriteLine ("    PADDING-TOP: 6px;")
txtstream.WriteLine ("    BORDER-BOTTOM: #999 1px solid;")
txtstream.WriteLine ("    BACKGROUND-COLOR: #eeeeee;")
txtstream.WriteLine ("    FONT-FAMILY: font-family: Cambria, serif;")
txtstream.WriteLine ("    FONT-SIZE: 12px;")
txtstream.WriteLine ("    text-align: left;")
txtstream.WriteLine ("    white-Space: nowrap;")
txtstream.WriteLine ("}")
```

```
txtstream.WriteLine (".th")
txtstream.WriteLine ("{")
txtstream.WriteLine ("    BORDER-RIGHT: #999999 2px solid;")
txtstream.WriteLine ("    PADDING-RIGHT: 6px;")
txtstream.WriteLine ("    PADDING-LEFT: 6px;")
txtstream.WriteLine ("    FONT-WEIGHT: Bold;")
txtstream.WriteLine ("    PADDING-BOTTOM: 6px;")
txtstream.WriteLine ("    COLOR: black;")
txtstream.WriteLine ("    PADDING-TOP: 6px;")
txtstream.WriteLine ("    BORDER-BOTTOM: #999 2px solid;")
txtstream.WriteLine ("    BACKGROUND-COLOR: #eeeeee;")
txtstream.WriteLine ("    FONT-FAMILY: font-family: Cambria, serif;")
txtstream.WriteLine ("    FONT-SIZE: 10px;")
txtstream.WriteLine ("    text-align: right;")
txtstream.WriteLine ("    white-Space: nowrap;")
txtstream.WriteLine ("}")
txtstream.WriteLine ("td")
txtstream.WriteLine ("{")
txtstream.WriteLine ("    BORDER-RIGHT: #999999 3px solid;")
txtstream.WriteLine ("    PADDING-RIGHT: 6px;")
txtstream.WriteLine ("    PADDING-LEFT: 6px;")
txtstream.WriteLine ("    FONT-WEIGHT: Normal;")
txtstream.WriteLine ("    PADDING-BOTTOM: 6px;")
txtstream.WriteLine ("    COLOR: navy;")
txtstream.WriteLine ("    LINE-HEIGHT: 14px;")
txtstream.WriteLine ("    PADDING-TOP: 6px;")
txtstream.WriteLine ("    BORDER-BOTTOM: #999 1px solid;")
txtstream.WriteLine ("    BACKGROUND-COLOR: #eeeeee;")
txtstream.WriteLine ("    FONT-FAMILY: font-family: Cambria, serif;")
txtstream.WriteLine ("    FONT-SIZE: 12px;")
txtstream.WriteLine ("    text-align: left;")
txtstream.WriteLine ("    white-Space: nowrap;")
txtstream.WriteLine ("}")
```

```
txtstream.WriteLine ("div")
txtstream.WriteLine ("{")
txtstream.WriteLine ("    BORDER-RIGHT: #999999 3px solid;")
txtstream.WriteLine ("    PADDING-RIGHT: 6px;")
txtstream.WriteLine ("    PADDING-LEFT: 6px;")
txtstream.WriteLine ("    FONT-WEIGHT: Normal;")
txtstream.WriteLine ("    PADDING-BOTTOM: 6px;")
txtstream.WriteLine ("    COLOR: white;")
txtstream.WriteLine ("    PADDING-TOP: 6px;")
txtstream.WriteLine ("    BORDER-BOTTOM: #999 1px solid;")
txtstream.WriteLine ("    BACKGROUND-COLOR: navy;")
txtstream.WriteLine ("    FONT-FAMILY: font-family: Cambria, serif;")
txtstream.WriteLine ("    FONT-SIZE: 10px;")
txtstream.WriteLine ("    text-align: left;")
txtstream.WriteLine ("    white-Space: nowrap;")
txtstream.WriteLine ("}")
txtstream.WriteLine ("span")
txtstream.WriteLine ("{")
txtstream.WriteLine ("    BORDER-RIGHT: #999999 3px solid;")
txtstream.WriteLine ("    PADDING-RIGHT: 3px;")
txtstream.WriteLine ("    PADDING-LEFT: 3px;")
txtstream.WriteLine ("    FONT-WEIGHT: Normal;")
txtstream.WriteLine ("    PADDING-BOTTOM: 3px;")
txtstream.WriteLine ("    COLOR: white;")
txtstream.WriteLine ("    PADDING-TOP: 3px;")
txtstream.WriteLine ("    BORDER-BOTTOM: #999 1px solid;")
txtstream.WriteLine ("    BACKGROUND-COLOR: navy;")
txtstream.WriteLine ("    FONT-FAMILY: font-family: Cambria, serif;")
txtstream.WriteLine ("    FONT-SIZE: 10px;")
txtstream.WriteLine ("    text-align: left;")
txtstream.WriteLine ("    white-Space: nowrap;")
txtstream.WriteLine ("    display: inline-block;")
txtstream.WriteLine ("    width: 100%;")
```

txtstream.WriteLine ("}")

txtstream.WriteLine ("textarea")

txtstream.WriteLine ("{")

txtstream.WriteLine ("   BORDER-RIGHT: #999999 3px solid;")

txtstream.WriteLine ("   PADDING-RIGHT: 3px;")

txtstream.WriteLine ("   PADDING-LEFT: 3px;")

txtstream.WriteLine ("   FONT-WEIGHT: Normal;")

txtstream.WriteLine ("   PADDING-BOTTOM: 3px;")

txtstream.WriteLine ("   COLOR: white;")

txtstream.WriteLine ("   PADDING-TOP: 3px;")

txtstream.WriteLine ("   BORDER-BOTTOM: #999 1px solid;")

txtstream.WriteLine ("   BACKGROUND-COLOR: navy;")

txtstream.WriteLine ("   FONT-FAMILY: font-family: Cambria, serif;")

txtstream.WriteLine ("   FONT-SIZE: 10px;")

txtstream.WriteLine ("   text-align: left;")

txtstream.WriteLine ("   white-Space: nowrap;")

txtstream.WriteLine ("   width: 100%;")

txtstream.WriteLine ("}")

txtstream.WriteLine ("select")

txtstream.WriteLine ("{")

txtstream.WriteLine ("   BORDER-RIGHT: #999999 3px solid;")

txtstream.WriteLine ("   PADDING-RIGHT: 6px;")

txtstream.WriteLine ("   PADDING-LEFT: 6px;")

txtstream.WriteLine ("   FONT-WEIGHT: Normal;")

txtstream.WriteLine ("   PADDING-BOTTOM: 6px;")

txtstream.WriteLine ("   COLOR: white;")

txtstream.WriteLine ("   PADDING-TOP: 6px;")

txtstream.WriteLine ("   BORDER-BOTTOM: #999 1px solid;")

txtstream.WriteLine ("   BACKGROUND-COLOR: navy;")

txtstream.WriteLine ("   FONT-FAMILY: font-family: Cambria, serif;")

txtstream.WriteLine ("   FONT-SIZE: 10px;")

txtstream.WriteLine ("   text-align: left;")

txtstream.WriteLine ("   white-Space: nowrap;")

```
txtstream.WriteLine ("   width: 100%;")
txtstream.WriteLine ("}")
txtstream.WriteLine ("input")
txtstream.WriteLine ("{")
txtstream.WriteLine ("   BORDER-RIGHT: #999999 3px solid;")
txtstream.WriteLine ("   PADDING-RIGHT: 3px;")
txtstream.WriteLine ("   PADDING-LEFT: 3px;")
txtstream.WriteLine ("   FONT-WEIGHT: Bold;")
txtstream.WriteLine ("   PADDING-BOTTOM: 3px;")
txtstream.WriteLine ("   COLOR: white;")
txtstream.WriteLine ("   PADDING-TOP: 3px;")
txtstream.WriteLine ("   BORDER-BOTTOM: #999 1px solid;")
txtstream.WriteLine ("   BACKGROUND-COLOR: navy;")
txtstream.WriteLine ("   FONT-FAMILY: font-family: Cambria, serif;")
txtstream.WriteLine ("   FONT-SIZE: 12px;")
txtstream.WriteLine ("   text-align: left;")
txtstream.WriteLine ("   display: table-cell;")
txtstream.WriteLine ("   white-Space: nowrap;")
txtstream.WriteLine ("   width: 100%;")
txtstream.WriteLine ("}")
txtstream.WriteLine ("h1 {")
txtstream.WriteLine ("color: antiquewhite;")
txtstream.WriteLine ("text-shadow: 1px 1px 1px black;")
txtstream.WriteLine ("padding: 3px;")
txtstream.WriteLine ("text-align: center;")
txtstream.WriteLine ("box-shadow: inset 2px 2px 5px rgba(0,0,0,0.5),
inset -2px -2px 5px rgba(255,255,255,0.5)")
txtstream.WriteLine ("}")
txtstream.WriteLine ("</style>")
txtstream.WriteLine ("</head>")
txtstream.WriteLine ("<body>")
txtstream.WriteLine ("<%")
```

```
        txtstream.WriteLine ("Response.Write(""<table Border='1' cellpadding='1'
cellspacing='1'>"" & vbcrlf)")

        Select Case Orientation

        Case "Single-Line Horizontal"

                txtstream.WriteLine ("Response.Write(""<tr>"" & vbcrlf)")
                For x = 0 To Names.Count -1
                    txtstream.WriteLine ("Response.Write(""<th>" + Names.Item(x)
+ "</th>"" & vbcrlf)")
                Next
                txtstream.WriteLine ("Response.Write(""</tr>"" & vbcrlf)")
                txtstream.WriteLine ("Response.Write(""<tr>"" & vbcrlf)")
                For x = 0 To Names.Count -1
                    txtstream.WriteLine          ("Response.Write(""<td>"          +
Rows.Item(y)(x) + "</td>"" & vbcrlf)")
                Next
                txtstream.WriteLine ("Response.Write(""</tr>"" & vbcrlf)")


        Case "Multi-Line Horizontal"

                txtstream.WriteLine ("Response.Write(""<tr>"" & vbcrlf)")
                For x = 0 To Names.Count -1
                    txtstream.WriteLine ("Response.Write(""<th>" + Names.Item(x)
+ "</th>"" & vbcrlf)")
                Next
                txtstream.WriteLine ("Response.Write(""</tr>"" & vbcrlf)")
                For y = 0 To  Rows.Count -1
                    txtstream.WriteLine ("Response.Write(""<tr>"" & vbcrlf)")
                    For x = 0 To Names.Count -1
                        txtstream.WriteLine          ("Response.Write(""<td>"          +
Rows.Item(y)(x) + "</td>"" & vbcrlf)")
```

```vb
                Next
                txtstream.WriteLine ("Response.Write(""</tr>"" & vbcrlf)")
            Next

        Case "Single-Line Vertical"

            For x = 0 To Names.Count -1
                txtstream.WriteLine          ("Response.Write(""<tr> <th>"          +
Names.Item(x) + "</th><td>" + Rows.Item(y)(x) + "</td></tr>"" & vbcrlf)")
            Next

        Case "Multi-Line Vertical"

            For x = 0 To Names.Count -1
                txtstream.WriteLine          ("Response.Write(""<tr><th>"          +
Names.Item(x) + "</th>"" & vbcrlf)")
                For y = 0 To Row.Count-1
                    txtstream.WriteLine          ("Response.Write(""<td>"          +
Rows.Item(y)(x) + "</td>"" & vbcrlf)")
                Next
                txtstream.WriteLine ("Response.Write(""</tr>"" & vbcrlf)")
            Next

        End Select
        txtstream.WriteLine ("Response.Write(""</table>"" & vbcrlf)")
        txtstream.WriteLine ("%>")
        txtstream.WriteLine ("</body>")
        txtstream.WriteLine ("</html>")
        txtstream.Close

    End                                                                        Sub
```

CREATE HTA CODE

Inside this sub routine is the code to create an HTA Application. You simply pass in the collection generated by the Return_Management_Collection and specify its orientation.

```
Public Sub Create_HTA_Code()

    Set ws = CreateObject("WScript.Shell")
    Set fso = CreateObject("Scripting.FileSystemObject")
    Set    txtstream    =    fso.OpenTextFile(ws.CurrentDirectory    +
"\\Win32_Process.hta", 2, True, -2)
    txtstream.WriteLine ("<html>")
    txtstream.WriteLine ("<head>")
    txtstream.WriteLine ("<HTA:APPLICATION ")
    txtstream.WriteLine ("ID = ""Process"" ")
    txtstream.WriteLine ("APPLICATIONNAME = ""Process"" ")
    txtstream.WriteLine ("SCROLL = ""yes"" ")
    txtstream.WriteLine ("SINGLEINSTANCE = ""yes"" ")
    txtstream.WriteLine ("WINDOWSTATE = ""maximize"" >")
    txtstream.WriteLine ("<title>Win32_Process</title>")
    txtstream.WriteLine ("<style type='text/css'>")
    txtstream.WriteLine ("body")
    txtstream.WriteLine ("{")
    txtstream.WriteLine ("    PADDING-RIGHT: 0px;")
    txtstream.WriteLine ("    PADDING-LEFT: 0px;")
    txtstream.WriteLine ("    PADDING-BOTTOM: 0px;")
    txtstream.WriteLine ("    MARGIN: 0px;")
    txtstream.WriteLine ("    COLOR: #333;")
    txtstream.WriteLine ("    PADDING-TOP: 0px;")
```

txtstream.WriteLine ("   FONT-FAMILY: verdana, arial, helvetica, sans-serif;")

txtstream.WriteLine ("}")

txtstream.WriteLine ("table")

txtstream.WriteLine ("{")

txtstream.WriteLine ("   BORDER-RIGHT: #999999 1px solid;")

txtstream.WriteLine ("   PADDING-RIGHT: 1px;")

txtstream.WriteLine ("   PADDING-LEFT: 1px;")

txtstream.WriteLine ("   PADDING-BOTTOM: 1px;")

txtstream.WriteLine ("   LINE-HEIGHT: 8px;")

txtstream.WriteLine ("   PADDING-TOP: 1px;")

txtstream.WriteLine ("   BORDER-BOTTOM: #999 1px solid;")

txtstream.WriteLine ("   BACKGROUND-COLOR: #eeeeee;")

txtstream.WriteLine ("   filter:progid:DXImageTransform.Microsoft.Shadow(color='silver',   Direction=135, Strength=16)")

txtstream.WriteLine ("}")

txtstream.WriteLine ("th")

txtstream.WriteLine ("{")

txtstream.WriteLine ("   BORDER-RIGHT: #999999 3px solid;")

txtstream.WriteLine ("   PADDING-RIGHT: 6px;")

txtstream.WriteLine ("   PADDING-LEFT: 6px;")

txtstream.WriteLine ("   FONT-WEIGHT: Bold;")

txtstream.WriteLine ("   FONT-SIZE: 14px;")

txtstream.WriteLine ("   PADDING-BOTTOM: 6px;")

txtstream.WriteLine ("   COLOR: darkred;")

txtstream.WriteLine ("   LINE-HEIGHT: 14px;")

txtstream.WriteLine ("   PADDING-TOP: 6px;")

txtstream.WriteLine ("   BORDER-BOTTOM: #999 1px solid;")

txtstream.WriteLine ("   BACKGROUND-COLOR: #eeeeee;")

txtstream.WriteLine ("   FONT-FAMILY: font-family: Cambria, serif;")

txtstream.WriteLine ("   FONT-SIZE: 12px;")

txtstream.WriteLine ("   text-align: left;")

txtstream.WriteLine ("   white-Space: nowrap;")

txtstream.WriteLine ("}")

txtstream.WriteLine (".th")

txtstream.WriteLine ("{")

txtstream.WriteLine ("   BORDER-RIGHT: #999999 2px solid;")

txtstream.WriteLine ("   PADDING-RIGHT: 6px;")

txtstream.WriteLine ("   PADDING-LEFT: 6px;")

txtstream.WriteLine ("   FONT-WEIGHT: Bold;")

txtstream.WriteLine ("   PADDING-BOTTOM: 6px;")

txtstream.WriteLine ("   COLOR: black;")

txtstream.WriteLine ("   PADDING-TOP: 6px;")

txtstream.WriteLine ("   BORDER-BOTTOM: #999 2px solid;")

txtstream.WriteLine ("   BACKGROUND-COLOR: #eeeeee;")

txtstream.WriteLine ("   FONT-FAMILY: font-family: Cambria, serif;")

txtstream.WriteLine ("   FONT-SIZE: 10px;")

txtstream.WriteLine ("   text-align: right;")

txtstream.WriteLine ("   white-Space: nowrap;")

txtstream.WriteLine ("}")

txtstream.WriteLine ("td")

txtstream.WriteLine ("{")

txtstream.WriteLine ("   BORDER-RIGHT: #999999 3px solid;")

txtstream.WriteLine ("   PADDING-RIGHT: 6px;")

txtstream.WriteLine ("   PADDING-LEFT: 6px;")

txtstream.WriteLine ("   FONT-WEIGHT: Normal;")

txtstream.WriteLine ("   PADDING-BOTTOM: 6px;")

txtstream.WriteLine ("   COLOR: navy;")

txtstream.WriteLine ("   LINE-HEIGHT: 14px;")

txtstream.WriteLine ("   PADDING-TOP: 6px;")

txtstream.WriteLine ("   BORDER-BOTTOM: #999 1px solid;")

txtstream.WriteLine ("   BACKGROUND-COLOR: #eeeeee;")

txtstream.WriteLine ("   FONT-FAMILY: font-family: Cambria, serif;")

txtstream.WriteLine ("   FONT-SIZE: 12px;")

txtstream.WriteLine ("   text-align: left;")

```
txtstream.WriteLine ("    white-Space: nowrap;")
txtstream.WriteLine ("}")
txtstream.WriteLine ("div")
txtstream.WriteLine ("{")
txtstream.WriteLine ("    BORDER-RIGHT: #999999 3px solid;")
txtstream.WriteLine ("    PADDING-RIGHT: 6px;")
txtstream.WriteLine ("    PADDING-LEFT: 6px;")
txtstream.WriteLine ("    FONT-WEIGHT: Normal;")
txtstream.WriteLine ("    PADDING-BOTTOM: 6px;")
txtstream.WriteLine ("    COLOR: white;")
txtstream.WriteLine ("    PADDING-TOP: 6px;")
txtstream.WriteLine ("    BORDER-BOTTOM: #999 1px solid;")
txtstream.WriteLine ("    BACKGROUND-COLOR: navy;")
txtstream.WriteLine ("    FONT-FAMILY: font-family: Cambria, serif;")
txtstream.WriteLine ("    FONT-SIZE: 10px;")
txtstream.WriteLine ("    text-align: left;")
txtstream.WriteLine ("    white-Space: nowrap;")
txtstream.WriteLine ("}")
txtstream.WriteLine ("span")
txtstream.WriteLine ("{")
txtstream.WriteLine ("    BORDER-RIGHT: #999999 3px solid;")
txtstream.WriteLine ("    PADDING-RIGHT: 3px;")
txtstream.WriteLine ("    PADDING-LEFT: 3px;")
txtstream.WriteLine ("    FONT-WEIGHT: Normal;")
txtstream.WriteLine ("    PADDING-BOTTOM: 3px;")
txtstream.WriteLine ("    COLOR: white;")
txtstream.WriteLine ("    PADDING-TOP: 3px;")
txtstream.WriteLine ("    BORDER-BOTTOM: #999 1px solid;")
txtstream.WriteLine ("    BACKGROUND-COLOR: navy;")
txtstream.WriteLine ("    FONT-FAMILY: font-family: Cambria, serif;")
txtstream.WriteLine ("    FONT-SIZE: 10px;")
txtstream.WriteLine ("    text-align: left;")
txtstream.WriteLine ("    white-Space: nowrap;")
```

```
txtstream.WriteLine ("    display: inline-block;")
txtstream.WriteLine ("    width: 100%;")
txtstream.WriteLine ("}")
txtstream.WriteLine ("textarea")
txtstream.WriteLine ("{")
txtstream.WriteLine ("    BORDER-RIGHT: #999999 3px solid;")
txtstream.WriteLine ("    PADDING-RIGHT: 3px;")
txtstream.WriteLine ("    PADDING-LEFT: 3px;")
txtstream.WriteLine ("    FONT-WEIGHT: Normal;")
txtstream.WriteLine ("    PADDING-BOTTOM: 3px;")
txtstream.WriteLine ("    COLOR: white;")
txtstream.WriteLine ("    PADDING-TOP: 3px;")
txtstream.WriteLine ("    BORDER-BOTTOM: #999 1px solid;")
txtstream.WriteLine ("    BACKGROUND-COLOR: navy;")
txtstream.WriteLine ("    FONT-FAMILY: font-family: Cambria, serif;")
txtstream.WriteLine ("    FONT-SIZE: 10px;")
txtstream.WriteLine ("    text-align: left;")
txtstream.WriteLine ("    white-Space: nowrap;")
txtstream.WriteLine ("    width: 100%;")
txtstream.WriteLine ("}")
txtstream.WriteLine ("select")
txtstream.WriteLine ("{")
txtstream.WriteLine ("    BORDER-RIGHT: #999999 3px solid;")
txtstream.WriteLine ("    PADDING-RIGHT: 6px;")
txtstream.WriteLine ("    PADDING-LEFT: 6px;")
txtstream.WriteLine ("    FONT-WEIGHT: Normal;")
txtstream.WriteLine ("    PADDING-BOTTOM: 6px;")
txtstream.WriteLine ("    COLOR: white;")
txtstream.WriteLine ("    PADDING-TOP: 6px;")
txtstream.WriteLine ("    BORDER-BOTTOM: #999 1px solid;")
txtstream.WriteLine ("    BACKGROUND-COLOR: navy;")
txtstream.WriteLine ("    FONT-FAMILY: font-family: Cambria, serif;")
txtstream.WriteLine ("    FONT-SIZE: 10px;")
```

```
txtstream.WriteLine ("    text-align: left;")
txtstream.WriteLine ("    white-Space: nowrap;")
txtstream.WriteLine ("    width: 100%;")
txtstream.WriteLine ("}")
txtstream.WriteLine ("input")
txtstream.WriteLine ("{")
txtstream.WriteLine ("    BORDER-RIGHT: #999999 3px solid;")
txtstream.WriteLine ("    PADDING-RIGHT: 3px;")
txtstream.WriteLine ("    PADDING-LEFT: 3px;")
txtstream.WriteLine ("    FONT-WEIGHT: Bold;")
txtstream.WriteLine ("    PADDING-BOTTOM: 3px;")
txtstream.WriteLine ("    COLOR: white;")
txtstream.WriteLine ("    PADDING-TOP: 3px;")
txtstream.WriteLine ("    BORDER-BOTTOM: #999 1px solid;")
txtstream.WriteLine ("    BACKGROUND-COLOR: navy;")
txtstream.WriteLine ("    FONT-FAMILY: font-family: Cambria, serif;")
txtstream.WriteLine ("    FONT-SIZE: 12px;")
txtstream.WriteLine ("    text-align: left;")
txtstream.WriteLine ("    display: table-cell;")
txtstream.WriteLine ("    white-Space: nowrap;")
txtstream.WriteLine ("    width: 100%;")
txtstream.WriteLine ("}")
txtstream.WriteLine ("h1 {")
txtstream.WriteLine ("color: antiquewhite;")
txtstream.WriteLine ("text-shadow: 1px 1px 1px black;")
txtstream.WriteLine ("padding: 3px;")
txtstream.WriteLine ("text-align: center;")
txtstream.WriteLine ("box-shadow: inset 2px 2px 5px rgba(0,0,0,0.5), inset -2px -2px 5px rgba(255,255,255,0.5)")
txtstream.WriteLine ("}")
txtstream.WriteLine ("</style>")
txtstream.WriteLine ("</head>")
txtstream.WriteLine ("<body>")
```

```
txtstream.WriteLine ("<table Border='1' cellpadding='1' cellspacing='1'>")

Select Case Orientation

    Case "Single-Line Horizontal"

        txtstream.WriteLine ("<tr>")
        For x = 0 To Names.Count -1
            txtstream.WriteLine ("<th>" + Names.Item(x) + "</th>")
        Next
        txtstream.WriteLine ("</tr>")
        txtstream.WriteLine ("<tr>")
        For x = 0 To Names.Count -1
            txtstream.WriteLine ("<td>" + Rows.Item(y)(x) + "</td>")
        Next
        txtstream.WriteLine ("</tr>")

    Case "Multi-Line Horizontal"

        txtstream.WriteLine ("<tr>")
        For x = 0 To Names.Count -1
            txtstream.WriteLine ("<th>" + Names.Item(x) + "</th>")
        Next
        txtstream.WriteLine ("</tr>")
        For y = 0 To  Rows.Count -1
            txtstream.WriteLine ("<tr>")
            For x = 0 To Names.Count -1
                txtstream.WriteLine ("<td>" + Rows.Item(y)(x) + "</td>")
        Next
            txtstream.WriteLine ("</tr>")
        Next

    Case "Single-Line Vertical"
```

```
            For x = 0 To Names.Count –1
                txtstream.WriteLine      ("<tr><th>"      +      Names.Item(x)      +
"</th><td>" + Rows.Item(y)(x) + "</td></tr>")
            Next

        Case "Multi–Line Vertical"

            For x = 0 To Names.Count –1
                txtstream.WriteLine ("<tr><th>" + Names.Item(x) + "</th>")
                For y = 0 To Row.Count–1
                    txtstream.WriteLine ("<td>" + Rows.Item(y)(x) + "</td>")
                Next
                txtstream.WriteLine ("</tr>")
            Next

    End Select
    txtstream.WriteLine ("</table>")
    txtstream.WriteLine ("</body>")
    txtstream.WriteLine ("</html>")
    txtstream.Close

End                                                                        Sub
```

CREATE HTML CODE

Inside this sub routine is the code to create an HTML Webpage that can be saved and displayed using the Web Browser control or saved and displayed at a later time.

You simply pass in the collection generated by the Return_Management_Collection and specify its orientation.

```
Public Sub Create_HTML_Code()

    Set ws = CreateObject("WScript.Shell")
    Set fso = CreateObject("Scripting.FileSystemObject")
    Set txtstream = fso.OpenTextFile(ws.CurrentDirectory +
"\\Win32_Process.html", 2, True, -2)
    txtstream.WriteLine ("<html>")
    txtstream.WriteLine ("<head>")
    txtstream.WriteLine ("<title>Win32_Process</title>")
    txtstream.WriteLine ("<style type='text/css'>")
    txtstream.WriteLine ("body")
    txtstream.WriteLine ("{")
    txtstream.WriteLine ("   PADDING-RIGHT: 0px;")
    txtstream.WriteLine ("   PADDING-LEFT: 0px;")
    txtstream.WriteLine ("   PADDING-BOTTOM: 0px;")
    txtstream.WriteLine ("   MARGIN: 0px;")
    txtstream.WriteLine ("   COLOR: #333;")
    txtstream.WriteLine ("   PADDING-TOP: 0px;")
    txtstream.WriteLine ("   FONT-FAMILY: verdana, arial, helvetica, sans-
serif;")
    txtstream.WriteLine ("}")
    txtstream.WriteLine ("table")
    txtstream.WriteLine ("{")
    txtstream.WriteLine ("   BORDER-RIGHT: #999999 1px solid;")
```

```
txtstream.WriteLine ("   PADDING-RIGHT: 1px;")
txtstream.WriteLine ("   PADDING-LEFT: 1px;")
txtstream.WriteLine ("   PADDING-BOTTOM: 1px;")
txtstream.WriteLine ("   LINE-HEIGHT: 8px;")
txtstream.WriteLine ("   PADDING-TOP: 1px;")
txtstream.WriteLine ("   BORDER-BOTTOM: #999 1px solid;")
txtstream.WriteLine ("   BACKGROUND-COLOR: #eeeeee;")
txtstream.WriteLine                                          ("
filter:progid:DXImageTransform.Microsoft.Shadow(color='silver',   Direction=135,
Strength=16)")
txtstream.WriteLine ("}")
txtstream.WriteLine ("th")
txtstream.WriteLine ("{")
txtstream.WriteLine ("   BORDER-RIGHT: #999999 3px solid;")
txtstream.WriteLine ("   PADDING-RIGHT: 6px;")
txtstream.WriteLine ("   PADDING-LEFT: 6px;")
txtstream.WriteLine ("   FONT-WEIGHT: Bold;")
txtstream.WriteLine ("   FONT-SIZE: 14px;")
txtstream.WriteLine ("   PADDING-BOTTOM: 6px;")
txtstream.WriteLine ("   COLOR: darkred;")
txtstream.WriteLine ("   LINE-HEIGHT: 14px;")
txtstream.WriteLine ("   PADDING-TOP: 6px;")
txtstream.WriteLine ("   BORDER-BOTTOM: #999 1px solid;")
txtstream.WriteLine ("   BACKGROUND-COLOR: #eeeeee;")
txtstream.WriteLine ("   FONT-FAMILY: font-family: Cambria, serif;")
txtstream.WriteLine ("   FONT-SIZE: 12px;")
txtstream.WriteLine ("   text-align: left;")
txtstream.WriteLine ("   white-Space: nowrap;")
txtstream.WriteLine ("}")
txtstream.WriteLine (".th")
txtstream.WriteLine ("{")
txtstream.WriteLine ("   BORDER-RIGHT: #999999 2px solid;")
txtstream.WriteLine ("   PADDING-RIGHT: 6px;")
```

```
txtstream.WriteLine ("   PADDING-LEFT: 6px;")
txtstream.WriteLine ("   FONT-WEIGHT: Bold;")
txtstream.WriteLine ("   PADDING-BOTTOM: 6px;")
txtstream.WriteLine ("   COLOR: black;")
txtstream.WriteLine ("   PADDING-TOP: 6px;")
txtstream.WriteLine ("   BORDER-BOTTOM: #999 2px solid;")
txtstream.WriteLine ("   BACKGROUND-COLOR: #eeeeee;")
txtstream.WriteLine ("   FONT-FAMILY: font-family: Cambria, serif;")
txtstream.WriteLine ("   FONT-SIZE: 10px;")
txtstream.WriteLine ("   text-align: right;")
txtstream.WriteLine ("   white-Space: nowrap;")
txtstream.WriteLine ("}")
txtstream.WriteLine ("td")
txtstream.WriteLine ("{")
txtstream.WriteLine ("   BORDER-RIGHT: #999999 3px solid;")
txtstream.WriteLine ("   PADDING-RIGHT: 6px;")
txtstream.WriteLine ("   PADDING-LEFT: 6px;")
txtstream.WriteLine ("   FONT-WEIGHT: Normal;")
txtstream.WriteLine ("   PADDING-BOTTOM: 6px;")
txtstream.WriteLine ("   COLOR: navy;")
txtstream.WriteLine ("   LINE-HEIGHT: 14px;")
txtstream.WriteLine ("   PADDING-TOP: 6px;")
txtstream.WriteLine ("   BORDER-BOTTOM: #999 1px solid;")
txtstream.WriteLine ("   BACKGROUND-COLOR: #eeeeee;")
txtstream.WriteLine ("   FONT-FAMILY: font-family: Cambria, serif;")
txtstream.WriteLine ("   FONT-SIZE: 12px;")
txtstream.WriteLine ("   text-align: left;")
txtstream.WriteLine ("   white-Space: nowrap;")
txtstream.WriteLine ("}")
txtstream.WriteLine ("div")
txtstream.WriteLine ("{")
txtstream.WriteLine ("   BORDER-RIGHT: #999999 3px solid;")
txtstream.WriteLine ("   PADDING-RIGHT: 6px;")
```

```
txtstream.WriteLine ("    PADDING-LEFT: 6px;")
txtstream.WriteLine ("    FONT-WEIGHT: Normal;")
txtstream.WriteLine ("    PADDING-BOTTOM: 6px;")
txtstream.WriteLine ("    COLOR: white;")
txtstream.WriteLine ("    PADDING-TOP: 6px;")
txtstream.WriteLine ("    BORDER-BOTTOM: #999 1px solid;")
txtstream.WriteLine ("    BACKGROUND-COLOR: navy;")
txtstream.WriteLine ("    FONT-FAMILY: font family: Cambria, serif,")
txtstream.WriteLine ("    FONT-SIZE: 10px;")
txtstream.WriteLine ("    text-align: left;")
txtstream.WriteLine ("    white-Space: nowrap;")
txtstream.WriteLine ("}")
txtstream.WriteLine ("span")
txtstream.WriteLine ("{")
txtstream.WriteLine ("    BORDER-RIGHT: #999999 3px solid;")
txtstream.WriteLine ("    PADDING-RIGHT: 3px;")
txtstream.WriteLine ("    PADDING-LEFT: 3px;")
txtstream.WriteLine ("    FONT-WEIGHT: Normal;")
txtstream.WriteLine ("    PADDING-BOTTOM: 3px;")
txtstream.WriteLine ("    COLOR: white;")
txtstream.WriteLine ("    PADDING-TOP: 3px;")
txtstream.WriteLine ("    BORDER-BOTTOM: #999 1px solid;")
txtstream.WriteLine ("    BACKGROUND-COLOR: navy;")
txtstream.WriteLine ("    FONT-FAMILY: font-family: Cambria, serif;")
txtstream.WriteLine ("    FONT-SIZE: 10px;")
txtstream.WriteLine ("    text-align: left;")
txtstream.WriteLine ("    white-Space: nowrap;")
txtstream.WriteLine ("    display: inline-block;")
txtstream.WriteLine ("    width: 100%;")
txtstream.WriteLine ("}")
txtstream.WriteLine ("textarea")
txtstream.WriteLine ("{")
txtstream.WriteLine ("    BORDER-RIGHT: #999999 3px solid;")
```

```
txtstream.WriteLine ("    PADDING-RIGHT: 3px;")
txtstream.WriteLine ("    PADDING-LEFT: 3px;")
txtstream.WriteLine ("    FONT-WEIGHT: Normal;")
txtstream.WriteLine ("    PADDING-BOTTOM: 3px;")
txtstream.WriteLine ("    COLOR: white;")
txtstream.WriteLine ("    PADDING-TOP: 3px;")
txtstream.WriteLine ("    BORDER-BOTTOM: #999 1px solid;")
txtstream.WriteLine ("    BACKGROUND-COLOR: navy;")
txtstream.WriteLine ("    FONT-FAMILY: font-family: Cambria, serif;")
txtstream.WriteLine ("    FONT-SIZE: 10px;")
txtstream.WriteLine ("    text-align: left;")
txtstream.WriteLine ("    white-Space: nowrap;")
txtstream.WriteLine ("    width: 100%;")
txtstream.WriteLine ("}")
txtstream.WriteLine ("select")
txtstream.WriteLine ("{")
txtstream.WriteLine ("    BORDER-RIGHT: #999999 3px solid;")
txtstream.WriteLine ("    PADDING-RIGHT: 6px;")
txtstream.WriteLine ("    PADDING-LEFT: 6px;")
txtstream.WriteLine ("    FONT-WEIGHT: Normal;")
txtstream.WriteLine ("    PADDING-BOTTOM: 6px;")
txtstream.WriteLine ("    COLOR: white;")
txtstream.WriteLine ("    PADDING-TOP: 6px;")
txtstream.WriteLine ("    BORDER-BOTTOM: #999 1px solid;")
txtstream.WriteLine ("    BACKGROUND-COLOR: navy;")
txtstream.WriteLine ("    FONT-FAMILY: font-family: Cambria, serif;")
txtstream.WriteLine ("    FONT-SIZE: 10px;")
txtstream.WriteLine ("    text-align: left;")
txtstream.WriteLine ("    white-Space: nowrap;")
txtstream.WriteLine ("    width: 100%;")
txtstream.WriteLine ("}")
txtstream.WriteLine ("input")
txtstream.WriteLine ("{")
```

```
txtstream.WriteLine ("    BORDER-RIGHT: #999999 3px solid;")
txtstream.WriteLine ("    PADDING-RIGHT: 3px;")
txtstream.WriteLine ("    PADDING-LEFT: 3px;")
txtstream.WriteLine ("    FONT-WEIGHT: Bold;")
txtstream.WriteLine ("    PADDING-BOTTOM: 3px;")
txtstream.WriteLine ("    COLOR: white;")
txtstream.WriteLine ("    PADDING-TOP: 3px;")
txtstream.WriteLine ("    BORDER-BOTTOM: #999 1px solid;")
txtstream.WriteLine ("    BACKGROUND-COLOR: navy;")
txtstream.WriteLine ("    FONT-FAMILY: font-family: Cambria, serif;")
txtstream.WriteLine ("    FONT-SIZE: 12px;")
txtstream.WriteLine ("    text-align: left;")
txtstream.WriteLine ("    display: table-cell;")
txtstream.WriteLine ("    white-Space: nowrap;")
txtstream.WriteLine ("    width: 100%;")
txtstream.WriteLine ("}")
txtstream.WriteLine ("h1 {")
txtstream.WriteLine ("color: antiquewhite;")
txtstream.WriteLine ("text-shadow: 1px 1px 1px black;")
txtstream.WriteLine ("padding: 3px;")
txtstream.WriteLine ("text-align: center;")
txtstream.WriteLine ("box-shadow: inset 2px 2px 5px rgba(0,0,0,0.5),
inset -2px -2px 5px rgba(255,255,255,0.5)")
txtstream.WriteLine ("}")
txtstream.WriteLine ("</style>")
txtstream.WriteLine ("</head>")
txtstream.WriteLine ("<body>")
txtstream.WriteLine ("<table Border='1' cellpadding='1' cellspacing='1'>")

Select Case Orientation

    Case "Single-Line Horizontal"
```

```
        txtstream.WriteLine ("<tr>")
        For x = 0 To Names.Count -1
            txtstream.WriteLine ("<th>" + Names.Item(x) + "</th>")
        Next
        txtstream.WriteLine ("</tr>")
        txtstream.WriteLine ("<tr>")
        For x = 0 To Names.Count -1
            txtstream.WriteLine ("<td>" + Rows.Item(y)(x) + "</td>")
        Next
        txtstream.WriteLine ("</tr>")


    Case "Multi-Line Horizontal"

        txtstream.WriteLine ("<tr>")
        For x = 0 To Names.Count -1
            txtstream.WriteLine ("<th>" + Names.Item(x) + "</th>")
        Next
        txtstream.WriteLine ("</tr>")
        For y = 0 To  Rows.Count -1
            txtstream.WriteLine ("<tr>")
            For x = 0 To Names.Count -1
                txtstream.WriteLine ("<td>" + Rows.Item(y)(x) + "</td>")
        Next
            txtstream.WriteLine ("</tr>")
        Next


    Case "Single-Line Vertical"

        For x = 0 To Names.Count -1
            txtstream.WriteLine     ("<tr><th>"     +     Names.Item(x)     +
"</th><td>" + Rows.Item(y)(x) + "</td></tr>")
            Next
```

```
       Case "Multi-Line Vertical"

          For x = 0 To Names.Count -1
             txtstream.WriteLine ("<tr><th>" + Names.Item(x) + "</th>")
             For y = 0 To Row.Count-1
                txtstream.WriteLine ("<td>" + Rows.Item(y)(x) + "</td>")
             Next
             txtstream.WriteLine ("</tr>")
          Next

       End Select

       txtstream.WriteLine ("</table>")
       txtstream.WriteLine ("</body>")
       txtstream.WriteLine ("</html>")
       txtstream.Close


    End                                                    Sub
```

CREATE THE CSV FILE

Inside this sub routine is the code to create a CSV file. It is a separate routine because its extension -.csv – is seen by Excel – assuming it is installed as a text-based data file and knows what to do with it to display its contents.

You simply pass in the collection generated by the Return_Management_Collection and specify its orientation.

```
Public Sub Create_CSV_File_Code()

    Set ws = CreateObject("WScript.Shell")
    Set fso = CreateObject("Scripting.FileSystemObject")
    Set txtstream = fso.OpenTextFile(ws.CurrentDirectory &
"\\Win32_Process.csv", 2, True, -2)

    tempstr = ""

    Select Case Orientation

      Case "Horizontal"

          For x = 0 To Names.Count -1
            If tempstr <> "" Then
              tempstr = tempstr + ","
            End If
            tempstr = tempstr + prop.Name


          Next
          txtstream.WriteLine (tempstr)
```

```
        tempstr = ""
        For y = 0 to Rows.Count-1
            For x = 0 To Names.Count -1
                If tempstr <> "" Then
                    tempstr = tempstr + ","
                End If
                tempstr = tempstr + Chr(34) + Rows.Item(y)(x) + Chr(34)
            Next
            txtstream.WriteLine (tempstr)
            tempstr = ""
        Next
        txtstream.Close

    Case "Vertical"

        For x = 0 To Names.Count -1
            tempstr = prop.Name
            For y = 0 to Rows.Count-1
                If tempstr <> "" Then
                    tempstr = tempstr + ","
                End If
                tempstr = tempstr + Chr(34) + Rows.Item(y)(x)  + Chr(34)
            Next
            txtstream.WriteLine (tempstr)
            tempstr = ""
        Next

    End Select

    End                                                     Sub
```

CREATE THE EXCEL FILE

Inside this sub routine is the code to create a CSV file and then open it using an older version of Excel.

```
Public Sub Create_Excel_File_Code()

    Set ws = CreateObject("WScript.Shell")
    Set fso = CreateObject("Scripting.FileSystemObject")
    Set    txtstream    =    fso.OpenTextFile(ws.CurrentDirectory    &
"\\Win32_Process.csv", 2, True, -2)

    tempstr = ""

    Select Case Orientation

      Case "Horizontal"

          For x = 0 To Names.Count -1
            If tempstr <> "" Then
              tempstr = tempstr + ","
            End If
            tempstr = tempstr + prop.Name


          Next
          txtstream.WriteLine (tempstr)
          tempstr = ""
          For y = 0 to Rows.Count-1
```

```
         For x = 0 To Names.Count -1
            If tempstr <> "" Then
               tempstr = tempstr + ","
            End If
            tempstr = tempstr + Chr(34) + Rows.Item(y)(x) + Chr(34)
         Next
         txtstream.WriteLine (tempstr)
         tempstr = ""
      Next
      txtstream.Close

   Case "Vertical"

      For x = 0 To Names.Count -1
         tempstr = prop.Name
         For y = 0 to Rows.Count-1
            If tempstr <> "" Then
               tempstr = tempstr + ","
            End If
            tempstr = tempstr + Chr(34) + Rows.Item(y)(x)  + Chr(34)
         Next
         txtstream.WriteLine (tempstr)
         tempstr = ""
      Next
      txtstream.Close


   End Select

Dim ws As Object = CreateObject("Wscript.Shell")
ws.Run(Application.StartupPath & "\\Win32_Process.csv")

End Sub
```

EXCEL AUTOMATION CODE

Inside this sub routine is the code to create an instance of Excel and populate a worksheet. Both horizontal and vertical orientations are available, and the code automatically aligns and autofits the cells.

```
Set oexcel = CreateObject("Excel.Applicaiton")
Set wb = oexcel.WorkBooks.Add()
Set ws = wb.Worksheets(1)
ws.Name = "Win32_Process"

Select Case Orientation

  Case "Horizontal"

      For x = 0 To Names.Count -1
        ws.Cells(1, x+1) = prop.Name
        x = x + 1
      Next
      x = 1

      For y = 0 To Rows.Count-1
        For x = 0 To Names.Count -1
          ws.Cells(y+2, x+1) = Rows(y)(x)
        x = x + 1
        Next
        x = 1
        y = y + 1
      Next

  Case "Vertical"
```

```vba
    For x = 0 To Names.Count -1
        ws.Cells(x+1, 1) = prop.Name
        x = x + 1
    Next
    x = 1

    For y = 0 To Rows.Count-1
        For x = 0 To Names.Count -1
            ws.Cells(x+1, y +2) = Rows(y)(x)
        x = x + 1
        Next
        x = 1
        y = y + 1
    Next

End Select

ws.Columns.HorizontalAlignment = -4131
ws.Columns.Autofit


End                                                                 Sub
```

CREATE CUSTOM DELIMITED TEXT FILE

This sub routine is designed to provide you with maximum flexibility. You choose the orientation and the delimiter.

```
Public Sub Create_Text_File_Code()


    Set ws = CreateObject("WScript.Shell")
    Set fso = CreateObject("Scripting.FileSystemObject")
    Set txtstream = fso.OpenTextFile(ws.CurrentDirectory & "\\Win32_Process.txt", 2, True, -2)

    tempstr = ""

    Select Case Orientation

      Case "Horizontal"

            For x = 0 To Names.Count -1
              If tempstr <> "" Then
                tempstr = tempstr + delim
              End If
              tempstr = tempstr + prop.Name


            Next
            txtstream.WriteLine (tempstr)
```

```
        tempstr = ""
    For y = 0 to Rows.Count-1
       For x = 0 To Names.Count -1
          If tempstr <> "" Then
             tempstr = tempstr + delim
          End If
          tempstr = tempstr + Chr(34) + Rows.Item(y)(x) + Chr(34)
       Next
       txtstream.WriteLine (tempstr)
       tempstr = ""
    Next
    txtstream.Close


 Case "Vertical"


    For x = 0 To Names.Count -1
       tempstr = prop.Name
       For y = 0 to Rows.Count-1
           If tempstr <> "" Then
             tempstr = tempstr + delim
          End If
          tempstr = tempstr + Chr(34) + Rows.Item(y)(x)  + Chr(34)
       Next
       txtstream.WriteLine (tempstr)
       tempstr = ""
    Next
    txtstream.Close


 End Select



 End Sub
```

CREATE AN EXCEL
SPREADSHEET TEXT FILE

Simply put, this routine creates an Excel Spreadsheet File that will automatically be displayed by Excel as a worksheet.

```
Public Sub Create_Excel_SpreadSheet(ByVal objs)


    Set ws = CreateObject("WScript.Shell")
    Set fso = CreateObject("Scripting.FileSystemObject")
    Set txtstream = fso.OpenTextFile(ws.CurrentDirectory +
"\\ProcessExcel.xml", 2, True, -2)
        txtstream.WriteLine ("<?xml version='1.0'?>")
        txtstream.WriteLine ("<?mso-application progid='Excel.Sheet'?>")
        txtstream.WriteLine    ("<Workbook    xmlns='urn:schemas-microsoft-
com:office:spreadsheet'        xmlns:o='urn:schemas-microsoft-com:office:office'
xmlns:x='urn:schemas-microsoft-com:office:excel'        xmlns:ss='urn:schemas-
microsoft-com:office:spreadsheet'        xmlns:html='http://www.w3.org/TR/REC-
html40'>")
        txtstream.WriteLine ("    <Documentproperties xmlns='urn:schemas-
microsoft-com:office:office'>")
        txtstream.WriteLine ("    <Author>Windows User</Author>")
        txtstream.WriteLine ("    <LastAuthor>Windows User</LastAuthor>")
        txtstream.WriteLine ("    <Created>2007-11-27T19:36:16Z</Created>")
        txtstream.WriteLine ("    <Version>12.00</Version>")
        txtstream.WriteLine ("    </Documentproperties>")
```

```
txtstream.WriteLine  ("        <ExcelWorkbook   xmlns='urn:schemas-
microsoft-com:office:excel'>")
        txtstream.WriteLine ("    <WindowHeight>11835</WindowHeight>")
        txtstream.WriteLine ("    <WindowWidth>18960</WindowWidth>")
        txtstream.WriteLine ("    <WindowTopX>120</WindowTopX>")
        txtstream.WriteLine ("    <WindowTopY>135</WindowTopY>")
        txtstream.WriteLine ("    <ProtectStructure>False</ProtectStructure>")
        txtstream.WriteLine ("    <ProtectWindows>False</ProtectWindows> ")
        txtstream.WriteLine ("  </ExcelWorkbook>")
        txtstream.WriteLine ("  <Styles>")
        txtstream.WriteLine ("    <Style ss:ID='Default' ss:Name='Normal'>")
        txtstream.WriteLine ("      <Alignment ss:Vertical='Bottom'/>")
        txtstream.WriteLine ("      <Borders/>")
        txtstream.WriteLine  ("                    <Font   ss:FontName='Calibri'
x:Family='Swiss' ss:Size='11' ss:Color='#000000'/>")
        txtstream.WriteLine ("      <Interior/>")
        txtstream.WriteLine ("      <NumberFormat/>")
        txtstream.WriteLine ("      <Protection/>")
        txtstream.WriteLine ("    </Style>")
        txtstream.WriteLine ("    <Style ss:ID='s62'>")
        txtstream.WriteLine ("      <Borders/>")
        txtstream.WriteLine  ("                    <Font   ss:FontName='Calibri'
x:Family='Swiss' ss:Size='11' ss:Color='#000000' ss:Bold='1'/>")
        txtstream.WriteLine ("    </Style>")
        txtstream.WriteLine ("    <Style ss:ID='s63'>")
        txtstream.WriteLine  ("                 <Alignment  ss:Horizontal='Left'
ss:Vertical='Bottom' ss:Indent='2'/>")
        txtstream.WriteLine  ("                 <Font  ss:FontName='Verdana'
x:Family='Swiss' ss:Size='7.7' ss:Color='#000000'/>")
        txtstream.WriteLine ("    </Style>")
        txtstream.WriteLine ("  </Styles>")
        txtstream.WriteLine ("<Worksheet ss:Name='Process'>")
```

```vb
        txtstream.WriteLine ("          <Table  x:FullColumns='1'   x:FullRows='1'
ss:DefaultRowHeight='24.9375'>")
        txtstream.WriteLine ("        <Column ss:AutoFitWidth='1' ss:Width='82.5'
ss:Span='5'/>")

        txtstream.WriteLine ("     <Row ss:AutoFitHeight='0'>")
        For x = 0 To Names.Count -1
            txtstream.WriteLine ("                     <Cell ss:StyleID='s62'><Data
ss:Type='String'>" + Names.Item(x) + "</Data></Cell>")
        Next
        txtstream.WriteLine ("     </Row>")
        For y = 0 To Rows.Count -1
            txtstream.WriteLine ("                     <Row   ss:AutoFitHeight='0'
ss:Height='13.5'>")
            For x = 0 To Names.Count -1
                txtstream.WriteLine ("                          <Cell><Data
ss:Type='String'><![CDATA[" + Rows(y)(x) + "]]></Data></Cell>")
            Next
            txtstream.WriteLine ("     </Row>")
        Next
        txtstream.WriteLine (" </Table>")
        txtstream.WriteLine ("      <WorksheetOptions  xmlns='urn:schemas-
microsoft-com:office:excel'>")
        txtstream.WriteLine ("    <PageSetup>")
        txtstream.WriteLine ("     <Header x:Margin='0.3'/>")
        txtstream.WriteLine ("     <Footer x:Margin='0.3'/>")
        txtstream.WriteLine ("       <PageMargins x:Bottom='0.75' x:Left='0.7'
x:Right='0.7' x:Top='0.75'/>")
        txtstream.WriteLine ("    </PageSetup>")
        txtstream.WriteLine ("    <Unsynced/>")
        txtstream.WriteLine ("    <Print>")
        txtstream.WriteLine ("     <FitHeight>0</FitHeight>")
        txtstream.WriteLine ("     <ValidPrinterInfo/>")
```

```
        txtstream.WriteLine                                    ("
<HorizontalResolution>600</HorizontalResolution>")
        txtstream.WriteLine                                    ("
<VerticalResolution>600</VerticalResolution>")
        txtstream.WriteLine ("    </Print>")
        txtstream.WriteLine ("    <Selected/>")
        txtstream.WriteLine ("    <Panes>")
        txtstream.WriteLine ("      <Pane>")
        txtstream.WriteLine ("        <Number>3</Number>")
        txtstream.WriteLine ("        <ActiveRow>9</ActiveRow>")
        txtstream.WriteLine ("        <ActiveCol>7</ActiveCol>")
        txtstream.WriteLine ("      </Pane>")
        txtstream.WriteLine ("    </Panes>")
        txtstream.WriteLine ("    <ProtectObjects>False</ProtectObjects>")
        txtstream.WriteLine ("    <ProtectScenarios>False</ProtectScenarios>")
        txtstream.WriteLine ("  </WorksheetOptions>")
        txtstream.WriteLine ("</Worksheet>")
        txtstream.WriteLine ("</Workbook>")
        txtstream.Close

        Call ws.Run(ws.CurrentDirectory & "\ProcessExcel.xml")

    End                                                        Sub
```

CREATE AN XML FILE

This sub routine creates a very simple Element XML File. This file can be used with the MSDAOSP and therefore, becomes as database text file.

```
Public Sub Create_Element_XML_File_Code(ByVal objs)

    Set ws = CreateObject("WScript.Shell")
    Set fso = CreateObject("Scripting.FileSystemObject")
    Set     txtstream     =     fso.OpenTextFile(ws.CurrentDirectory     +
"\\Win32_Process.xml", 2, True, -2)
    txtstream.WriteLine ("<?xml version='1.0' encoding='iso-8859-1'?>")
    txtstream.WriteLine ("<data>")
    For y = 0 To Rows.Count-1
        txtstream.WriteLine ("<Win32_process>")
        For x = 0 To Names.Count -1
            txtstream.WriteLine ("<" + Names.Item(x) + ">" + Rows.Item(y)(x) +
"</" + Names.Item(x) + ">")
        Next
        txtstream.WriteLine ("</Win32_process>")
    Next
    txtstream.WriteLine ("</data>")
    txtstream.Close

    End                                                                    Sub
```

CREATE AN XML FOR XSL FILE

This sub routine creates a very simple Element XML File but is dependent upon the specified XSL file. This file cannot be used with the MSDAOSP due to its dependency on the XSL file.

```
Public Sub Create_Element_XML_For_XSL_Files_Code(ByVal objs)


    Set ws = CreateObject("WScript.Shell")
    Set fso = CreateObject("Scripting.FileSystemObject")
    Set    txtstream    =    fso.OpenTextFile(ws.CurrentDirectory    +
"\\Win32_Process.xml", 2, True, -2)
    txtstream.WriteLine ("<?xml version='1.0' encoding='iso-8859-1'?>")
    txtstream.WriteLine    ("<?xml-stylesheet    type='Text/xsl'    href='"    +
ws.CurrentDirectory + "\\Win32_Process.xsl'?>")
    txtstream.WriteLine ("<data>")
    For y = 0 To Rows.Count-1
       txtstream.WriteLine ("<Win32_process>")
       For x = 0 To Names.Count -1
          txtstream.WriteLine ("<" + Names.Item(x) + ">" + Rows.Item(y)(x) +
"</" + Names.Item(x) + ">")
       Next
       txtstream.WriteLine ("</Win32_process>")
    Next
    txtstream.WriteLine ("</data>")
    txtstream.Close


    End                                                               Sub
```

CREATE A SCHEMA XML

This sub routine creates a very simple Element XML File but is dependent upon the specified XSL file. It is opened by ADO and uses the MSDAOSP provider.

This file is then saved and can be used by the MSPERSIST provider.

```
Public Sub Create_Schema_XML_Files_Code(ByVal objs)

    Set ws = CreateObject("WScript.Shell")
    Set fso = CreateObject("Scripting.FileSystemObject")
    Set     txtstream     =     fso.OpenTextFile(ws.CurrentDirectory     +
"\\Win32_Process.xml", 2, True, -2)
    txtstream.WriteLine ("<?xml version='1.0' encoding='iso-8859-1'?>")
    txtstream.WriteLine ("<data>")
    For y = 0 To Rows.Count-1
       txtstream.WriteLine ("<Win32_process>")
       For x = 0 To Names.Count -1
          txtstream.WriteLine ("<" + Names.Item(x) + ">" + Rows.Item(y)(x) +
"</" + Names.Item(x) + ">")
       Next
       txtstream.WriteLine ("</Win32_process>")
    Next
    txtstream.WriteLine ("</data>")
    txtstream.Close

    Set ws = CreateObject("WScript.Shell")
    Set rs1 = CreateObject("ADODB.Recordset")
    rs1.ActiveConnection     =     "Provider=MSDAOSP;     Data
Source=msxml2.DSOControl"
    Call rs1.Open(ws.CurrentDirectory & "\\Win32_Process.xml")
```

```
        If  fso.FileExists(ws.CurrentDirectory  &  "\\Win32_Process_Schema.xml")
= True Then

            Call                    fso.DeleteFile(ws.CurrentDirectory            +
"\\Win32_Process_Schema.xml")
        End If

        Call rs1.Save(ws.CurrentDirectory & "\\Win32_Process_Schema.xml", 1)

    End                                                                    Sub
```

CREATE THE XSL FILES

Inside this sub routine is the code to create the XSL File designed to render the XML as an HTML Webpage. It can be saved and displayed using the Web Browser control or saved and displayed at a later time. Simply pass in the collection generated by the Return_Management_Collection and specify its orientation.

```
Public Sub Create_XSL_Files_Code()

Select Case Orientation

Case "SINGLE LINE HORIZONTAL"

        txtstream.WriteLine ("<?xml version='1.0' encoding='UTF-8'?>")
        txtstream.WriteLine            ("<xsl:stylesheet          version='1.0'
xmlns:xsl='http://www.w3.org/1999/XSL/Transform'>")
        txtstream.WriteLine ("<xsl:template match=""/"">")
        txtstream.WriteLine ("<html>")
        txtstream.WriteLine ("<head>")
        txtstream.WriteLine ("<title>Products</title>")
        txtstream.WriteLine ("<style type='text/css'>")
        txtstream.WriteLine ("th")
        txtstream.WriteLine ("{")
        txtstream.WriteLine ("   COLOR: darkred;")
        txtstream.WriteLine ("   BACKGROUND-COLOR: white;")
        txtstream.WriteLine ("        FONT-FAMILY:font-family: Cambria,
serif;")
        txtstream.WriteLine ("   FONT-SIZE: 12px;")
```

```
txtstream.WriteLine ("    text-align: left;")
txtstream.WriteLine ("    white-Space: nowrap;")
txtstream.WriteLine ("}")
txtstream.WriteLine ("td")
txtstream.WriteLine ("{")
txtstream.WriteLine ("    COLOR: navy;")
txtstream.WriteLine ("    BACKGROUND-COLOR: white;")
txtstream.WriteLine ("        FONT-FAMILY: font-family: Cambria, serif;")
txtstream.WriteLine ("    FONT-SIZE: 12px;")
txtstream.WriteLine ("    text-align: left;")
txtstream.WriteLine ("    white-Space: nowrap;")
txtstream.WriteLine ("}")
txtstream.WriteLine ("</style>")
txtstream.WriteLine ("</head>")
txtstream.WriteLine ("<body bgcolor='#333333'>")
txtstream.WriteLine ("<table colspacing='3' colpadding='3'>")
txtstream.WriteLine ("<tr>")
For x = 0 To Names.Count -1
    txtstream.WriteLine ("<th>" + Names.Item(x) + "</th>")
Next
txtstream.WriteLine ("</tr>")
txtstream.WriteLine ("<tr>")
For x = 0 To Names.Count -1
    txtstream.WriteLine                    ("<td><xsl:value-of
select=""data/Win32_Process/" & Names.Item(x) & """"/></td>")
Next
txtstream.WriteLine ("</tr>")
txtstream.WriteLine ("</table>")
txtstream.WriteLine ("</body>")
txtstream.WriteLine ("</html>")
txtstream.WriteLine ("</xsl:template>")
txtstream.WriteLine ("</xsl:stylesheet>")
```

```
        txtstream.Close


    Case "Multi Line Horizontal"


        txtstream.WriteLine ("<?xml version='1.0' encoding='UTF-8'?>")
        txtstream.WriteLine        ("<xsl:stylesheet        version='1.0'
xmlns:xsl='http://www.w3.org/1999/XSL/Transform'>")
        txtstream.WriteLine ("<xsl:template match=""/"">")
        txtstream.WriteLine ("<html>")
        txtstream.WriteLine ("<head>")
        txtstream.WriteLine ("<title>Products</title>")
        txtstream.WriteLine ("<style type='text/css'>")
        txtstream.WriteLine ("th")
        txtstream.WriteLine ("{")
        txtstream.WriteLine ("    COLOR: darkred;")
        txtstream.WriteLine ("    BACKGROUND-COLOR: white;")
        txtstream.WriteLine ("        FONT-FAMILY:font-family: Cambria,
serif;")
        txtstream.WriteLine ("    FONT-SIZE: 12px;")
        txtstream.WriteLine ("    text-align: left;")
        txtstream.WriteLine ("    white-Space: nowrap;")
        txtstream.WriteLine ("}")
        txtstream.WriteLine ("td")
        txtstream.WriteLine ("{")
        txtstream.WriteLine ("    COLOR: navy;")
        txtstream.WriteLine ("    BACKGROUND-COLOR: white;")
        txtstream.WriteLine ("        FONT-FAMILY: font-family: Cambria,
serif;")
        txtstream.WriteLine ("    FONT-SIZE: 12px;")
        txtstream.WriteLine ("    text-align: left;")
        txtstream.WriteLine ("    white-Space: nowrap;")
```

```
                txtstream.WriteLine ("}")
                txtstream.WriteLine ("</style>")
                txtstream.WriteLine ("</head>")
                txtstream.WriteLine ("<body bgcolor='#333333'>")
                txtstream.WriteLine ("<table colspacing='3' colpadding='3'>")
                txtstream.WriteLine ("<tr>")
                For x = 0 To Names.Count -1
                    txtstream.WriteLine ("<th>" + Names.Item(x) + "</th>")
                Next
                txtstream.WriteLine ("</tr>")
                txtstream.WriteLine                                    ("<xsl:for-each
select=""""data/Win32_Process"""">")
                txtstream.WriteLine ("<tr>")
                For x = 0 To Names.Count -1
                    txtstream.WriteLine                         ("<td><xsl:value-of
select=""""data/Win32_Process/" & Names.Item(x)  & """"/></td>")
                Next
                txtstream.WriteLine ("</tr>")
                txtstream.WriteLine ("</xsl:for-each>")
                txtstream.WriteLine ("</table>")
                txtstream.WriteLine ("</body>")
                txtstream.WriteLine ("</html>")
                txtstream.WriteLine ("</xsl:template>")
                txtstream.WriteLine ("</xsl:stylesheet>")
                txtstream.Close


            Case "Single Line Vertical"

                txtstream.WriteLine ("<?xml version='1.0' encoding='UTF-8'?>")
                txtstream.WriteLine              ("<xsl:stylesheet          version='1.0'
xmlns:xsl='http://www.w3.org/1999/XSL/Transform'>")
                txtstream.WriteLine ("<xsl:template match=""""/"""">")
```

```
txtstream.WriteLine ("<html>")
txtstream.WriteLine ("<head>")
txtstream.WriteLine ("<title>Products</title>")
txtstream.WriteLine ("<style type='text/css'>")
txtstream.WriteLine ("th")
txtstream.WriteLine ("{")
txtstream.WriteLine ("   COLOR: darkred;")
txtstream.WriteLine ("   BACKGROUND-COLOR: white;")
txtstream.WriteLine ("       FONT-FAMILY:font-family: Cambria,
serif;")
txtstream.WriteLine ("   FONT-SIZE: 12px;")
txtstream.WriteLine ("   text-align: left;")
txtstream.WriteLine ("   white-Space: nowrap;")
txtstream.WriteLine ("}")
txtstream.WriteLine ("td")
txtstream.WriteLine ("{")
txtstream.WriteLine ("   COLOR: navy;")
txtstream.WriteLine ("   BACKGROUND-COLOR: white;")
txtstream.WriteLine ("       FONT-FAMILY: font-family: Cambria,
serif;")
txtstream.WriteLine ("   FONT-SIZE: 12px;")
txtstream.WriteLine ("   text-align: left;")
txtstream.WriteLine ("   white-Space: nowrap;")
txtstream.WriteLine ("}")
txtstream.WriteLine ("</style>")
txtstream.WriteLine ("</head>")
txtstream.WriteLine ("<body bgcolor='#333333'>")
txtstream.WriteLine ("<table colspacing='3' colpadding='3'>")
For x = 0 To Names.Count -1
    txtstream.WriteLine ("<tr><th>" + Names.Item(x) + "</th>")
    txtstream.WriteLine ("<td><xsl:value-of
select=""data/Win32_Process/" + Names.Item(x) + """/></td></tr>")
Next
```

```
txtstream.WriteLine ("</table>")
txtstream.WriteLine ("</body>")
txtstream.WriteLine ("</html>")
txtstream.WriteLine ("</xsl:template>")
txtstream.WriteLine ("</xsl:stylesheet>")
txtstream.Close


    Case "Multi Line Vertical"

txtstream.WriteLine ("<?xml version='1.0' encoding='UTF-8'?>")
txtstream.WriteLine            ("<xsl:stylesheet            version='1.0'
xmlns:xsl='http://www.w3.org/1999/XSL/Transform'>")
txtstream.WriteLine ("<xsl:template match=""/"">")
txtstream.WriteLine ("<html>")
txtstream.WriteLine ("<head>")
txtstream.WriteLine ("<title>Products</title>")
txtstream.WriteLine ("<style type='text/css'>")
txtstream.WriteLine ("th")
txtstream.WriteLine ("{")
txtstream.WriteLine ("   COLOR: darkred;")
txtstream.WriteLine ("   BACKGROUND-COLOR: white;")
txtstream.WriteLine   ("        FONT-FAMILY:font-family:  Cambria,
serif;")
txtstream.WriteLine ("   FONT-SIZE: 12px;")
txtstream.WriteLine ("   text-align: left;")
txtstream.WriteLine ("   white-Space: nowrap;")
txtstream.WriteLine ("}")
txtstream.WriteLine ("td")
txtstream.WriteLine ("{")
txtstream.WriteLine ("   COLOR: navy;")
txtstream.WriteLine ("   BACKGROUND-COLOR: white;")
```

```vb
                txtstream.WriteLine ("        FONT-FAMILY: font-family: Cambria,
serif;")
                txtstream.WriteLine ("    FONT-SIZE: 12px;")
                txtstream.WriteLine ("    text-align: left;")
                txtstream.WriteLine ("    white-Space: nowrap;")
                txtstream.WriteLine ("}")
                txtstream.WriteLine ("</style>")
                txtstream.WriteLine ("</head>")
                txtstream.WriteLine ("<body bgcolor='#333333'>")
                txtstream.WriteLine ("<table colspacing='3' colpadding='3'>")
                For x = 0 To Names.Count -1
                    txtstream.WriteLine ("<tr><th>" + Names.Item(x) + "</th>")
                    txtstream.WriteLine ("<td><xsl:for-each
select=""""data/Win32_Process"""">")
                    txtstream.WriteLine ("<xsl:value-of select="""" + Names.Item(x) +
""""/></td>")
                    txtstream.WriteLine ("</xsl:for-each></tr>")
                Next
                txtstream.WriteLine ("</table>")
                txtstream.WriteLine ("</body>")
                txtstream.WriteLine ("</html>")
                txtstream.WriteLine ("</xsl:template>")
                txtstream.WriteLine ("</xsl:stylesheet>")
                txtstream.Close


        End Select

    End Sub
```

Stylesheets

The difference between boring and oh, wow!

The stylesheets in Appendix A, were used to render these pages. If you find one you like, feel free to use it.

Report:

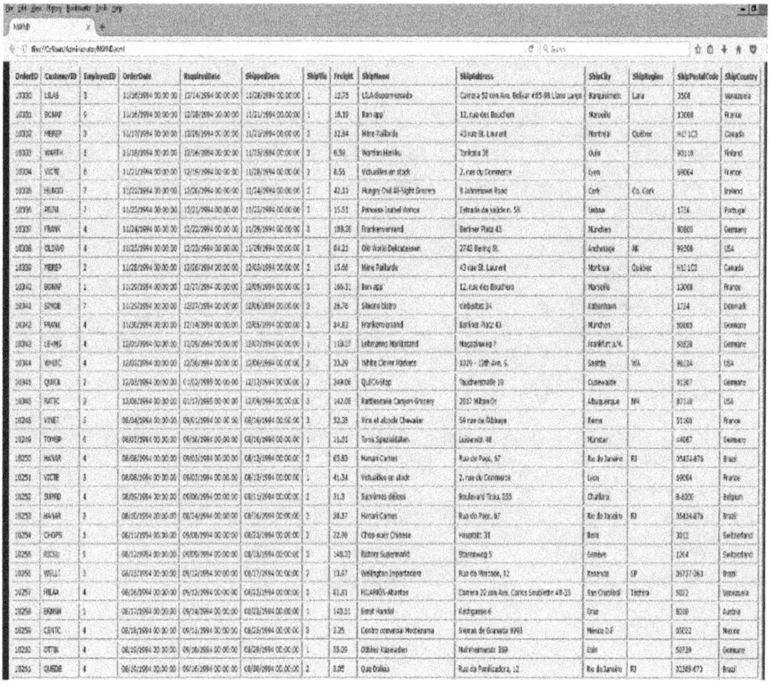

OrderID	CustomerID	EmployeeID	OrderDate	RequiredDate	ShippedDate	ShipVia	Freight	ShipName	ShipAddress	ShipCity	ShipRegion	ShipPostalCode	ShipCountry
10330	LILAS	3	11/16/1994 00:00:00	12/14/1994 00:00:00	11/28/1994 00:00:00	1	12.75	LILA-Supermercado	Carrera 52 con Ave. Bolívar #65-98 Llano Largo	Barquisimeto	Lara	3508	Venezuela
10331	BONAP	9	11/16/1994 00:00:00	12/28/1994 00:00:00	11/21/1994 00:00:00	1	10.19	Bon app'	12, rue des Bouchers	Marseille		13008	France
10332	MEREP	3	11/17/1994 00:00:00	12/29/1994 00:00:00	11/21/1994 00:00:00	2	52.84	Mère Paillarde	43 rue St. Laurent	Montréal	Québec	H1J 1C3	Canada
10333	WARTH	5	11/18/1994 00:00:00	12/16/1994 00:00:00	11/25/1994 00:00:00	3	0.59	Wartian Herkku	Torikatu 38	Oulu		90110	Finland
10334	VICTE	8	11/21/1994 00:00:00	12/19/1994 00:00:00	11/28/1994 00:00:00	2	8.56	Victuailles en stock	2, rue du Commerce	Lyon		69004	France
10335	HUNGO	7	11/22/1994 00:00:00	12/20/1994 00:00:00	11/24/1994 00:00:00	2	42.11	Hungry Owl All-Night Grocers	8 Johnstown Road	Cork	Co. Cork		Ireland
10336	PRINI	7	11/23/1994 00:00:00	12/21/1994 00:00:00	11/25/1994 00:00:00	2	15.51	Princesa Isabel Vinhos	Estrada da saúde n. 58	Lisboa		1756	Portugal
10337	FRANK	4	11/24/1994 00:00:00	12/22/1994 00:00:00	11/29/1994 00:00:00	3	108.26	Frankenversand	Berliner Platz 43	München		80805	Germany
10338	OLDWO	4	11/25/1994 00:00:00	12/23/1994 00:00:00	11/29/1994 00:00:00	3	84.21	Old World Delicatessen	2743 Bering St.	Anchorage	AK	99508	USA
10339	MEREP	2	11/28/1994 00:00:00	12/26/1994 00:00:00	12/05/1994 00:00:00	2	15.66	Mère Paillarde	43 rue St. Laurent	Montréal	Québec	H1J 1C3	Canada
10340	BONAP	1	11/29/1994 00:00:00	12/27/1994 00:00:00	12/09/1994 00:00:00	3	166.31	Bon app'	12, rue des Bouchers	Marseille		13008	France
10341	SIMOB	7	11/29/1994 00:00:00	12/27/1994 00:00:00	12/06/1994 00:00:00	3	26.78	Simons bistro	Vinbæltet 34	København		1734	Denmark
10342	FRANK	4	11/30/1994 00:00:00	12/14/1994 00:00:00	12/05/1994 00:00:00	2	54.83	Frankenversand	Berliner Platz 43	München		80805	Germany
10343	LEHMS	4	12/01/1994 00:00:00	12/29/1994 00:00:00	12/07/1994 00:00:00	1	110.37	Lehmanns Marktstand	Magazinweg 7	Frankfurt a.M.		60528	Germany
10344	WHITC	4	12/02/1994 00:00:00	12/30/1994 00:00:00	12/06/1994 00:00:00	2	23.29	White Clover Markets	1029 - 12th Ave. S.	Seattle	WA	98124	USA
10345	QUICK	2	12/05/1994 00:00:00	01/02/1995 00:00:00	12/12/1994 00:00:00	2	249.06	QUICK-Stop	Taucherstraße 10	Cunewalde		01307	Germany
10346	RATTC	3	12/06/1994 00:00:00	01/17/1995 00:00:00	12/09/1994 00:00:00	3	142.08	Rattlesnake Canyon Grocery	2817 Milton Dr.	Albuquerque	NM	87110	USA
10248	VINET	5	08/04/1994 00:00:00	09/01/1994 00:00:00	08/16/1994 00:00:00	3	32.38	Vins et alcools Chevalier	59 rue de l'Abbaye	Reims		51100	France
10249	TOMSP	6	08/05/1994 00:00:00	09/16/1994 00:00:00	08/10/1994 00:00:00	1	11.61	Toms Spezialitäten	Luisenstr. 48	Münster		44087	Germany
10250	HANAR	4	08/08/1994 00:00:00	09/05/1994 00:00:00	08/12/1994 00:00:00	2	65.83	Hanari Carnes	Rua do Paço, 67	Rio de Janeiro	RJ	05454-876	Brazil
10251	VICTE	3	08/08/1994 00:00:00	09/05/1994 00:00:00	08/15/1994 00:00:00	1	41.34	Victuailles en stock	2, rue du Commerce	Lyon		69004	France
10252	SUPRD	4	08/09/1994 00:00:00	09/06/1994 00:00:00	08/11/1994 00:00:00	2	51.3	Suprêmes délices	Boulevard Tirou, 255	Charleroi		B-6000	Belgium
10253	HANAR	3	08/10/1994 00:00:00	08/24/1994 00:00:00	08/16/1994 00:00:00	2	58.17	Hanari Carnes	Rua do Paço, 67	Rio de Janeiro	RJ	05454-876	Brazil
10254	CHOPS	5	08/11/1994 00:00:00	09/08/1994 00:00:00	08/23/1994 00:00:00	2	22.98	Chop-suey Chinese	Hauptstr. 31	Bern		3012	Switzerland
10255	RICSU	9	08/12/1994 00:00:00	09/09/1994 00:00:00	08/15/1994 00:00:00	3	148.33	Richter Supermarkt	Starenweg 5	Genève		1204	Switzerland
10256	WELLI	3	08/15/1994 00:00:00	09/12/1994 00:00:00	08/17/1994 00:00:00	2	13.97	Wellington Importadora	Rua do Mercado, 12	Resende	SP	08737-363	Brazil
10257	HILAA	4	08/16/1994 00:00:00	09/13/1994 00:00:00	08/22/1994 00:00:00	3	81.91	HILARIÓN-Abastos	Carrera 22 con Ave. Carlos Soublette #8-35	San Cristóbal	Táchira	5022	Venezuela
10258	ERNSH	1	08/17/1994 00:00:00	09/14/1994 00:00:00	08/23/1994 00:00:00	1	140.51	Ernst Handel	Kirchgasse 6	Graz		8010	Austria
10259	CENTC	4	08/18/1994 00:00:00	09/15/1994 00:00:00	08/25/1994 00:00:00	3	3.25	Centro comercial Moctezuma	Sierras de Granada 9993	México D.F.		05022	Mexico
10260	OTTIK	4	08/19/1994 00:00:00	09/16/1994 00:00:00	08/29/1994 00:00:00	1	55.09	Ottilies Käseladen	Mehrheimerstr. 369	Köln		50739	Germany
10261	QUEDE	4	08/19/1994 00:00:00	09/16/1994 00:00:00	08/30/1994 00:00:00	2	3.05	Que Delícia	Rua da Panificadora, 12	Rio de Janeiro	RJ	02389-673	Brazil

Table

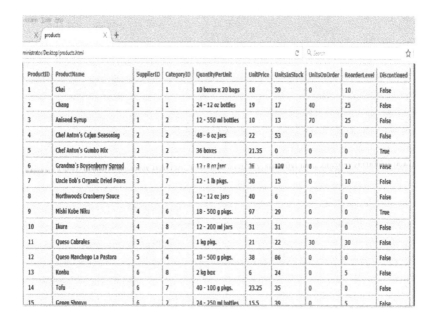

None:

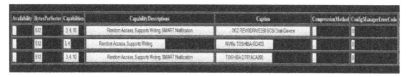

Black and White

Colored:

AccountExpires	AuthorizationFlags	BadPasswordCount	Caption	CodePage	Comment	CountryCode	Description
			NT AUTHORITY\SYSTEM				Network login profile settings for SYSTEM on NT AUTHORITY
			NT AUTHORITY\LOCAL SERVICE				Network login profile settings for LOCAL SERVICE on NT AUTHORITY
			NT AUTHORITY\NETWORK SERVICE				Network login profile settings for NETWORK SERVICE on NT AUTHORITY
	0	0	Administrator	0	Built-in account for administering the computer/domain	0	Network login profile settings for on WIN-8J8LOAKMFY8
			NT SERVICE\SQLTELEMETRY				Network login profile settings for SQLTELEMETRY on NT SERVICE
			NT SERVICE\SQLTELEMETRY$I39				Network login profile settings for SQLTELEMETRY$I39 on NT SERVICE
			NT SERVICE\SQLTELEMETRY				Network login profile settings for SQLTELEMETRY on NT SERVICE
			NT SERVICE\MSSQLServerOLAPService				Network login profile settings for MSSQLServerOLAPService on NT SERVICE
			NT SERVICE\ReportServer				Network login profile settings for ReportServer on NT SERVICE
			NT SERVICE\MSSQLFDLauncher				Network login profile settings for MSSQLFDLauncher on NT SERVICE
			NT SERVICE\MSSQLLaunchpad				Network login profile settings for MSSQLLaunchpad on NT SERVICE
			NT SERVICE\MsDtsServer130				Network login profile settings for MsDtsServer130 on NT SERVICE
			NT SERVICE\MSSQLSERVER				Network login profile settings for MSSQLSERVER on NT SERVICE
			IIS APPPOOL\Classic .NET AppPool				Network login profile settings for Classic .NET AppPool on IIS APPPOOL
			IIS APPPOOL\.NET v4.5				Network login profile settings for .NET v4.5 on IIS APPPOOL
			IIS APPPOOL\.NET v2.0				Network login profile settings for .NET v2.0 on IIS APPPOOL
			IIS APPPOOL\.NET v4.5 Classic				Network login profile settings for .NET v4.5 Classic on IIS APPPOOL
			IIS APPPOOL\.NET v2.0 Classic				Network login profile settings for .NET v2.0 Classic on IIS APPPOOL

Oscillating:

Availability	BytesPerSector	Capabilities	CapabilityDescriptions	Caption	CompressionMethod	ConfigManagerErrorCode	ConfigManagerUserConfig
	512	3, 4, 10	Random Access, Supports Writing, SMART Notification	OCZ REVODRIVE350 SCSI Disk Device		0	FALSE
	512	3, 4	Random Access, Supports Writing	NVMe TOSHIBA-RD400		0	FALSE
	512	3, 4, 10	Random Access, Supports Writing, SMART Notification	TOSHIBA DT01ACA200		0	FALSE

3D:

Availability	BytesPerSector	Capabilities	CapabilityDescriptions	Caption	CompressionMethod	ConfigManagerErrorCode	ConfigManagerUserConfig	CreationClassName
	512	3, 4, 10	Random Access, Supports Writing, SMART Notification	OCZ REVODRIVE350 SCSI Disk Device		0	FALSE	Win32_DiskDrive
	512	3, 4	Random Access, Supports Writing	NVMe TOSHIBA-RD400		0	FALSE	Win32_DiskDrive
	512	3, 4, 10	Random Access, Supports Writing, SMART Notification	TOSHIBA DT01ACA200		0	FALSE	Win32_DiskDrive

Shadow Box:

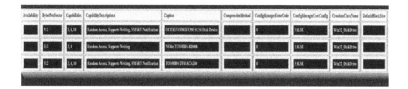

Availability	BytesPerSector	Capabilities	CapabilityDescriptions	Caption	CompressionMethod	ConfigManagerErrorCode	ConfigManagerUserConfig	CreationClassName	DefaultBlockSize
	512	3, 4, 10	Random Access, Supports Writing, SMART Notification	OCZ REVODRIVE350 SCSI Disk Device		0	FALSE	Win32_DiskDrive	
	512	3, 4	Random Access, Supports Writing	NVMe TOSHIBA-RD400		0	FALSE	Win32_DiskDrive	
	512	3, 4, 10	Random Access, Supports Writing, SMART Notification	TOSHIBA DT01ACA200		0	FALSE	Win32_DiskDrive	

Shadow Box Single Line Vertical

BiosCharacteristics	7, 10, 11, 12, 15, 16, 17, 19, 23, 24, 25, 26, 27, 28, 29, 32, 33, 40, 42, 43, 48, 50, 58, 59, 64, 65, 66, 67, 68, 69, 70, 71, 72, 73, 74, 75, 76, 77, 78, 79
BIOSVersion	ALASKA - 1072009, 0504, American Megatrends - 5000C
BuildNumber	
Caption	0504
CodeSet	
CurrentLanguage	en|US|iso8859-1
Description	0504
IdentificationCode	
InstallableLanguages	8
InstallDate	
LanguageEdition	
ListOfLanguages	en|US|iso8859-1, fr|FR|iso8859-1, zh|CN|unicode,,,,,
Manufacturer	American Megatrends Inc.
Name	0504
OtherTargetOS	
PrimaryBIOS	TRUE

Shadow Box Multi line Vertical

Availability			
BytesPerSector	512	512	512
Capabilities	3, 4, 10	3, 4	3, 4, 10
CapabilityDescriptions	Random Access, Supports Writing, SMART Notification	Random Access, Supports Writing	Random Access, Supports Writing, SMART Notification
Caption	OCZ-REVODRIVE350 SCSI Disk Device	NVMe TOSHIBA-RD400	TOSHIBA DT01ACA200
CompressionMethod			
ConfigManagerErrorCode	0	0	0
ConfigManagerUserConfig	FALSE	FALSE	FALSE
CreationClassName	Win32_DiskDrive	Win32_DiskDrive	Win32_DiskDrive
DefaultBlockSize			
Description	Disk drive	Disk drive	Disk drive
DeviceID	\\.\PHYSICALDRIVE2	\\.\PHYSICALDRIVE1	\\.\PHYSICALDRIVE0
ErrorCleared			
ErrorDescription			
ErrorMethodology			
FirmwareRevision	2.10	57CA012	MX6OABB0
Index	2	1	0

STYLESHEETS CODE

Decorating your web pages

BELOW ARE SOME STYLESHEETS I COOKED UP THAT I LIKE AND THINK YOU MIGHT TOO. Don't worry I won't be offended if you take and modify to your hearts delight. Please do!

NONE

```
txtstream.WriteLine("<style type='text/css'>")
txtstream.WriteLine("th")
txtstream.WriteLine("{")
txtstream.WriteLine("   COLOR: darkred;")
txtstream.WriteLine("}")
txtstream.WriteLine("td")
txtstream.WriteLine("{")
txtstream.WriteLine("   COLOR: Navy;")
txtstream.WriteLine("}")
txtstream.WriteLine("</style>")
```

BLACK AND WHITE TEXT

```
txtstream.WriteLine("<style type='text/css'>")
txtstream.WriteLine("th")
txtstream.WriteLine("{")
txtstream.WriteLine("   COLOR: white;")
txtstream.WriteLine("   BACKGROUND-COLOR: black;")
txtstream.WriteLine("   FONT-FAMILY:font-family: Cambria, serif;")
txtstream.WriteLine("   FONT-SIZE: 12px;")
```

```
txtstream.WriteLine("   text-align: left;")
txtstream.WriteLine("   white-Space: nowrap;")
txtstream.WriteLine("}")
txtstream.WriteLine("td")
txtstream.WriteLine("{")
txtstream.WriteLine("   COLOR: white;")
txtstream.WriteLine("   BACKGROUND-COLOR: black;")
txtstream.WriteLine("   FONT-FAMILY: font-family: Cambria, serif;")
txtstream.WriteLine("   FONT-SIZE: 12px;")
txtstream.WriteLine("   text-align: left;")
txtstream.WriteLine("   white-Space: nowrap;")
txtstream.WriteLine("}")
txtstream.WriteLine("div")
txtstream.WriteLine("{")
txtstream.WriteLine("   COLOR: white;")
txtstream.WriteLine("   BACKGROUND-COLOR: black;")
txtstream.WriteLine("   FONT-FAMILY: font-family: Cambria, serif;")
txtstream.WriteLine("   FONT-SIZE: 10px;")
txtstream.WriteLine("   text-align: left;")
txtstream.WriteLine("   white-Space: nowrap;")
txtstream.WriteLine("}")
txtstream.WriteLine("span")
txtstream.WriteLine("{")
txtstream.WriteLine("   COLOR: white;")
txtstream.WriteLine("   BACKGROUND-COLOR: black;")
txtstream.WriteLine("   FONT-FAMILY: font-family: Cambria, serif;")
txtstream.WriteLine("   FONT-SIZE: 10px;")
txtstream.WriteLine("   text-align: left;")
txtstream.WriteLine("   white-Space: nowrap;")
txtstream.WriteLine("   display:inline-block;")
txtstream.WriteLine("   width: 100%;")
txtstream.WriteLine("}")
txtstream.WriteLine("textarea")
```

```
txtstream.WriteLine("{")
txtstream.WriteLine("    COLOR: white;")
txtstream.WriteLine("    BACKGROUND-COLOR: black;")
txtstream.WriteLine("    FONT-FAMILY: font-family: Cambria, serif;")
txtstream.WriteLine("    FONT-SIZE: 10px;")
txtstream.WriteLine("    text-align: left;")
txtstream.WriteLine("    white-Space: nowrap;")
txtstream.WriteLine("    width: 100%;")
txtstream.WriteLine("}")
txtstream.WriteLine("select")
txtstream.WriteLine("{")
txtstream.WriteLine("    COLOR: white;")
txtstream.WriteLine("    BACKGROUND-COLOR: black;")
txtstream.WriteLine("    FONT-FAMILY: font-family: Cambria, serif;")
txtstream.WriteLine("    FONT-SIZE: 10px;")
txtstream.WriteLine("    text-align: left;")
txtstream.WriteLine("    white-Space: nowrap;")
txtstream.WriteLine("    width: 100%;")
txtstream.WriteLine("}")
txtstream.WriteLine("input")
txtstream.WriteLine("{")
txtstream.WriteLine("    COLOR: white;")
txtstream.WriteLine("    BACKGROUND-COLOR: black;")
txtstream.WriteLine("    FONT-FAMILY: font-family: Cambria, serif;")
txtstream.WriteLine("    FONT-SIZE: 12px;")
txtstream.WriteLine("    text-align: left;")
txtstream.WriteLine("    display:table-cell;")
txtstream.WriteLine("    white-Space: nowrap;")
txtstream.WriteLine("}")
txtstream.WriteLine("h1 {")
txtstream.WriteLine("color: antiquewhite;")
txtstream.WriteLine("text-shadow: 1px 1px 1px black;")
txtstream.WriteLine("padding: 3px;")
```

```
txtstream.WriteLine("text-align: center;")
txtstream.WriteLine("box-shadow: inset 2px 2px 5px rgba(0,0,0,0.5), inset -
2px -2px 5px rgba(255,255,255,0.5)")
txtstream.WriteLine("}")
txtstream.WriteLine("</style>")
```

COLORED TEXT

```
txtstream.WriteLine("<style type='text/css'>")
txtstream.WriteLine("th")
txtstream.WriteLine("{")
txtstream.WriteLine("   COLOR: darkred;")
txtstream.WriteLine("   BACKGROUND-COLOR: #eeeeee;")
txtstream.WriteLine("   FONT-FAMILY:font-family: Cambria, serif;")
txtstream.WriteLine("   FONT-SIZE: 12px;")
txtstream.WriteLine("   text-align: left;")
txtstream.WriteLine("   white-Space: nowrap;")
txtstream.WriteLine("}")
txtstream.WriteLine("td")
txtstream.WriteLine("{")
txtstream.WriteLine("   COLOR: navy;")
txtstream.WriteLine("   BACKGROUND-COLOR: #eeeeee;")
txtstream.WriteLine("   FONT-FAMILY: font-family: Cambria, serif;")
txtstream.WriteLine("   FONT-SIZE: 12px;")
txtstream.WriteLine("   text-align: left;")
txtstream.WriteLine("   white-Space: nowrap;")
txtstream.WriteLine("}")
txtstream.WriteLine("div")
txtstream.WriteLine("{")
txtstream.WriteLine("   COLOR: white;")
txtstream.WriteLine("   BACKGROUND-COLOR: navy;")
txtstream.WriteLine("   FONT-FAMILY: font-family: Cambria, serif;")
txtstream.WriteLine("   FONT-SIZE: 10px;")
```

```
txtstream.WriteLine("    text-align: left;")
txtstream.WriteLine("    white-Space: nowrap;")
txtstream.WriteLine("}")
txtstream.WriteLine("span")
txtstream.WriteLine("{")
txtstream.WriteLine("    COLOR: white;")
txtstream.WriteLine("    BACKGROUND-COLOR: navy;")
txtstream.WriteLine("    FONT-FAMILY: font-family: Cambria, serif;")
txtstream.WriteLine("    FONT-SIZE: 10px;")
txtstream.WriteLine("    text-align: left;")
txtstream.WriteLine("    white-Space: nowrap;")
txtstream.WriteLine("    display:inline-block;")
txtstream.WriteLine("    width: 100%;")
txtstream.WriteLine("}")
txtstream.WriteLine("textarea")
txtstream.WriteLine("{")
txtstream.WriteLine("    COLOR: white;")
txtstream.WriteLine("    BACKGROUND-COLOR: navy;")
txtstream.WriteLine("    FONT-FAMILY: font-family: Cambria, serif;")
txtstream.WriteLine("    FONT-SIZE: 10px;")
txtstream.WriteLine("    text-align: left;")
txtstream.WriteLine("    white-Space: nowrap;")
txtstream.WriteLine("    width: 100%;")
txtstream.WriteLine("}")
txtstream.WriteLine("select")
txtstream.WriteLine("{")
txtstream.WriteLine("    COLOR: white;")
txtstream.WriteLine("    BACKGROUND-COLOR: navy;")
txtstream.WriteLine("    FONT-FAMILY: font-family: Cambria, serif;")
txtstream.WriteLine("    FONT-SIZE: 10px;")
txtstream.WriteLine("    text-align: left;")
txtstream.WriteLine("    white-Space: nowrap;")
txtstream.WriteLine("    width: 100%;")
```

```
txtstream.WriteLine("}")
txtstream.WriteLine("input")
txtstream.WriteLine("{")
txtstream.WriteLine("   COLOR: white;")
txtstream.WriteLine("   BACKGROUND-COLOR: navy;")
txtstream.WriteLine("   FONT-FAMILY: font-family: Cambria, serif;")
txtstream.WriteLine("   FONT-SIZE: 12px;")
txtstream.WriteLine("   text-align: left;")
txtstream.WriteLine("   display:table-cell;")
txtstream.WriteLine("   white-Space: nowrap;")
txtstream.WriteLine("}")
txtstream.WriteLine("h1 {")
txtstream.WriteLine("color: antiquewhite;")
txtstream.WriteLine("text-shadow: 1px 1px 1px black;")
txtstream.WriteLine("padding: 3px;")
txtstream.WriteLine("text-align: center;")
txtstream.WriteLine("box-shadow: inset 2px 2px 5px rgba(0,0,0,0.5), inset -
2px -2px 5px rgba(255,255,255,0.5)")
txtstream.WriteLine("}")
txtstream.WriteLine("</style>")
```

OSCILLATING ROW COLORS

```
txtstream.WriteLine("<style>")
txtstream.WriteLine("th")
txtstream.WriteLine("{")
txtstream.WriteLine("   COLOR: white;")
txtstream.WriteLine("   BACKGROUND-COLOR: navy;")
txtstream.WriteLine("   FONT-FAMILY:font-family: Cambria, serif;")
txtstream.WriteLine("   FONT-SIZE: 12px;")
txtstream.WriteLine("   text-align: left;")
```

```
txtstream.WriteLine("    white-Space: nowrap;")
txtstream.WriteLine("}")
txtstream.WriteLine("td")
txtstream.WriteLine("{")
txtstream.WriteLine("    COLOR: navy;")
txtstream.WriteLine("    FONT-FAMILY: font-family: Cambria, serif;")
txtstream.WriteLine("    FONT-SIZE: 12px;")
txtstream.WriteLine("    text-align: left;")
txtstream.WriteLine("    white-Space: nowrap;")
txtstream.WriteLine("}")
txtstream.WriteLine("div")
txtstream.WriteLine("{")
txtstream.WriteLine("    COLOR: navy;")
txtstream.WriteLine("    FONT-FAMILY: font-family: Cambria, serif;")
txtstream.WriteLine("    FONT-SIZE: 12px;")
txtstream.WriteLine("    text-align: left;")
txtstream.WriteLine("    white-Space: nowrap;")
txtstream.WriteLine("}")
txtstream.WriteLine("span")
txtstream.WriteLine("{")
txtstream.WriteLine("    COLOR: navy;")
txtstream.WriteLine("    FONT-FAMILY: font-family: Cambria, serif;")
txtstream.WriteLine("    FONT-SIZE: 12px;")
txtstream.WriteLine("    text-align: left;")
txtstream.WriteLine("    white-Space: nowrap;")
txtstream.WriteLine("    width: 100%;")
txtstream.WriteLine("}")
txtstream.WriteLine("textarea")
txtstream.WriteLine("{")
txtstream.WriteLine("    COLOR: navy;")
txtstream.WriteLine("    FONT-FAMILY: font-family: Cambria, serif;")
txtstream.WriteLine("    FONT-SIZE: 12px;")
txtstream.WriteLine("    text-align: left;")
```

```
txtstream.WriteLine("    white-Space: nowrap;")
txtstream.WriteLine("    display:inline-block;")
txtstream.WriteLine("    width: 100%;")
txtstream.WriteLine("}")
txtstream.WriteLine("select")
txtstream.WriteLine("{")
txtstream.WriteLine("    COLOR: navy;")
txtstream.WriteLine("    FONT-FAMILY: font-family: Cambria, serif;")
txtstream.WriteLine("    FONT-SIZE: 10px;")
txtstream.WriteLine("    text-align: left;")
txtstream.WriteLine("    white-Space: nowrap;")
txtstream.WriteLine("    display:inline-block;")
txtstream.WriteLine("    width: 100%;")
txtstream.WriteLine("}")
txtstream.WriteLine("input")
txtstream.WriteLine("{")
txtstream.WriteLine("    COLOR: navy;")
txtstream.WriteLine("    FONT-FAMILY: font-family: Cambria, serif;")
txtstream.WriteLine("    FONT-SIZE: 12px;")
txtstream.WriteLine("    text-align: left;")
txtstream.WriteLine("    display:table-cell;")
txtstream.WriteLine("    white-Space: nowrap;")
txtstream.WriteLine("}")
txtstream.WriteLine("h1 {")
txtstream.WriteLine("color: antiquewhite;")
txtstream.WriteLine("text-shadow: 1px 1px 1px black;")
txtstream.WriteLine("padding: 3px;")
txtstream.WriteLine("text-align: center;")
txtstream.WriteLine("box-shadow: inset 2px 2px 5px rgba(0,0,0,0.5), inset -
2px -2px 5px rgba(255,255,255,0.5)")
txtstream.WriteLine("}")
txtstream.WriteLine("tr:nth-child(even){background-color:#f2f2f2;}")
```

```
txtstream.WriteLine("tr:nth-child(odd){background-color:#cccccc;
color:#f2f2f2;}")
txtstream.WriteLine("</style>")
```

GHOST DECORATED

```
txtstream.WriteLine("<style type='text/css'>")
txtstream.WriteLine("th")
txtstream.WriteLine("{")
txtstream.WriteLine("    COLOR: black;")
txtstream.WriteLine("    BACKGROUND-COLOR: white;")
txtstream.WriteLine("    FONT-FAMILY:font-family: Cambria, serif;")
txtstream.WriteLine("    FONT-SIZE: 12px;")
txtstream.WriteLine("    text-align: left;")
txtstream.WriteLine("    white-Space: nowrap;")
txtstream.WriteLine("}")
txtstream.WriteLine("td")
txtstream.WriteLine("{")
txtstream.WriteLine("    COLOR: black;")
txtstream.WriteLine("    BACKGROUND-COLOR: white;")
txtstream.WriteLine("    FONT-FAMILY: font-family: Cambria, serif;")
txtstream.WriteLine("    FONT-SIZE: 12px;")
txtstream.WriteLine("    text-align: left;")
txtstream.WriteLine("    white-Space: nowrap;")
txtstream.WriteLine("}")
txtstream.WriteLine("div")
txtstream.WriteLine("{")
txtstream.WriteLine("    COLOR: black;")
txtstream.WriteLine("    BACKGROUND-COLOR: white;")
txtstream.WriteLine("    FONT-FAMILY: font-family: Cambria, serif;")
txtstream.WriteLine("    FONT-SIZE: 10px;")
txtstream.WriteLine("    text-align: left;")
txtstream.WriteLine("    white-Space: nowrap;")
```

```
txtstream.WriteLine("}")
txtstream.WriteLine("span")
txtstream.WriteLine("{")
txtstream.WriteLine("   COLOR: black;")
txtstream.WriteLine("   BACKGROUND-COLOR: white;")
txtstream.WriteLine("   FONT-FAMILY: font-family: Cambria, serif;")
txtstream.WriteLine("   FONT-SIZE: 10px;")
txtstream.WriteLine("   text-align: left;")
txtstream.WriteLine("   white-Space: nowrap;")
txtstream.WriteLine("   display:inline-block;")
txtstream.WriteLine("   width: 100%;")
txtstream.WriteLine("}")
txtstream.WriteLine("textarea")
txtstream.WriteLine("{")
txtstream.WriteLine("   COLOR: black;")
txtstream.WriteLine("   BACKGROUND-COLOR: white;")
txtstream.WriteLine("   FONT-FAMILY: font-family: Cambria, serif;")
txtstream.WriteLine("   FONT-SIZE: 10px;")
txtstream.WriteLine("   text-align: left;")
txtstream.WriteLine("   white-Space: nowrap;")
txtstream.WriteLine("   width: 100%;")
txtstream.WriteLine("}")
txtstream.WriteLine("select")
txtstream.WriteLine("{")
txtstream.WriteLine("   COLOR: black;")
txtstream.WriteLine("   BACKGROUND-COLOR: white;")
txtstream.WriteLine("   FONT-FAMILY: font-family: Cambria, serif;")
txtstream.WriteLine("   FONT-SIZE: 10px;")
txtstream.WriteLine("   text-align: left;")
txtstream.WriteLine("   white-Space: nowrap;")
txtstream.WriteLine("   width: 100%;")
txtstream.WriteLine("}")
txtstream.WriteLine("input")
```

```
txtstream.WriteLine("{")
txtstream.WriteLine("   COLOR: black;")
txtstream.WriteLine("   BACKGROUND-COLOR: white;")
txtstream.WriteLine("   FONT-FAMILY: font-family: Cambria, serif;")
txtstream.WriteLine("   FONT-SIZE: 12px;")
txtstream.WriteLine("   text-align: left;")
txtstream.WriteLine("   display:table-cell;")
txtstream.WriteLine("   white-Space: nowrap;")
txtstream.WriteLine("}")
txtstream.WriteLine("h1 {")
txtstream.WriteLine("color: antiquewhite;")
txtstream.WriteLine("text-shadow: 1px 1px 1px black;")
txtstream.WriteLine("padding: 3px;")
txtstream.WriteLine("text-align: center;")
txtstream.WriteLine("box-shadow: inset 2px 2px 5px rgba(0,0,0,0.5), inset -2px -2px 5px rgba(255,255,255,0.5)")
txtstream.WriteLine("}")
txtstream.WriteLine("</style>")
```

3D

```
txtstream.WriteLine("<style type='text/css'>")
txtstream.WriteLine("body")
txtstream.WriteLine("{")
txtstream.WriteLine("   PADDING-RIGHT: 0px;")
txtstream.WriteLine("   PADDING-LEFT: 0px;")
txtstream.WriteLine("   PADDING-BOTTOM: 0px;")
txtstream.WriteLine("   MARGIN: 0px;")
txtstream.WriteLine("   COLOR: #333;")
txtstream.WriteLine("   PADDING-TOP: 0px;")
txtstream.WriteLine("   FONT-FAMILY: verdana, arial, helvetica, sans-serif;")
txtstream.WriteLine("}")
```

```
txtstream.WriteLine("table")
txtstream.WriteLine("{")
txtstream.WriteLine("   BORDER-RIGHT: #999999 3px solid;")
txtstream.WriteLine("   PADDING-RIGHT: 6px;")
txtstream.WriteLine("   PADDING-LEFT: 6px;")
txtstream.WriteLine("   FONT-WEIGHT: Bold;")
txtstream.WriteLine("   FONT-SIZE: 14px;")
txtstream.WriteLine("   PADDING-BOTTOM: 6px;")
txtstream.WriteLine("   COLOR: Peru;")
txtstream.WriteLine("   LINE-HEIGHT: 14px;")
txtstream.WriteLine("   PADDING-TOP: 6px;")
txtstream.WriteLine("   BORDER-BOTTOM: #999 1px solid;")
txtstream.WriteLine("   BACKGROUND-COLOR: #eeeeee;")
txtstream.WriteLine("   FONT-FAMILY: verdana, arial, helvetica, sans-serif;")
txtstream.WriteLine("   FONT-SIZE: 12px;")
txtstream.WriteLine("}")
txtstream.WriteLine("th")
txtstream.WriteLine("{")
txtstream.WriteLine("   BORDER-RIGHT: #999999 3px solid;")
txtstream.WriteLine("   PADDING-RIGHT: 6px;")
txtstream.WriteLine("   PADDING-LEFT: 6px;")
txtstream.WriteLine("   FONT-WEIGHT: Bold;")
txtstream.WriteLine("   FONT-SIZE: 14px;")
txtstream.WriteLine("   PADDING-BOTTOM: 6px;")
txtstream.WriteLine("   COLOR: darkred;")
txtstream.WriteLine("   LINE-HEIGHT: 14px;")
txtstream.WriteLine("   PADDING-TOP: 6px;")
txtstream.WriteLine("   BORDER-BOTTOM: #999 1px solid;")
txtstream.WriteLine("   BACKGROUND-COLOR: #eeeeee;")
txtstream.WriteLine("   FONT-FAMILY:font-family: Cambria, serif;")
txtstream.WriteLine("   FONT-SIZE: 12px;")
txtstream.WriteLine("   text-align: left;")
txtstream.WriteLine("   white-Space: nowrap;")
```

```
txtstream.WriteLine("}")
txtstream.WriteLine(".th")
txtstream.WriteLine("{")
txtstream.WriteLine("    BORDER-RIGHT: #999999 2px solid;")
txtstream.WriteLine("    PADDING-RIGHT: 6px;")
txtstream.WriteLine("    PADDING-LEFT: 6px;")
txtstream.WriteLine("    FONT-WEIGHT: Bold;")
txtstream.WriteLine("    PADDING-BOTTOM: 6px;")
txtstream.WriteLine("    COLOR: black;")
txtstream.WriteLine("    PADDING-TOP: 6px;")
txtstream.WriteLine("    BORDER-BOTTOM: #999 2px solid;")
txtstream.WriteLine("    BACKGROUND-COLOR: #eeeeee;")
txtstream.WriteLine("    FONT-FAMILY: font-family: Cambria, serif;")
txtstream.WriteLine("    FONT-SIZE: 10px;")
txtstream.WriteLine("    text-align: right;")
txtstream.WriteLine("    white-Space: nowrap;")
txtstream.WriteLine("}")
txtstream.WriteLine("td")
txtstream.WriteLine("{")
txtstream.WriteLine("    BORDER-RIGHT: #999999 3px solid;")
txtstream.WriteLine("    PADDING-RIGHT: 6px;")
txtstream.WriteLine("    PADDING-LEFT: 6px;")
txtstream.WriteLine("    FONT-WEIGHT: Normal;")
txtstream.WriteLine("    PADDING-BOTTOM: 6px;")
txtstream.WriteLine("    COLOR: navy;")
txtstream.WriteLine("    LINE-HEIGHT: 14px;")
txtstream.WriteLine("    PADDING-TOP: 6px;")
txtstream.WriteLine("    BORDER-BOTTOM: #999 1px solid;")
txtstream.WriteLine("    BACKGROUND-COLOR: #eeeeee;")
txtstream.WriteLine("    FONT-FAMILY: font-family: Cambria, serif;")
txtstream.WriteLine("    FONT-SIZE: 12px;")
txtstream.WriteLine("    text-align: left;")
txtstream.WriteLine("    white-Space: nowrap;")
```

```
txtstream.WriteLine("}")
txtstream.WriteLine("div")
txtstream.WriteLine("{")
txtstream.WriteLine("    BORDER-RIGHT: #999999 3px solid;")
txtstream.WriteLine("    PADDING-RIGHT: 6px;")
txtstream.WriteLine("    PADDING-LEFT: 6px;")
txtstream.WriteLine("    FONT-WEIGHT: Normal;")
txtstream.WriteLine("    PADDING-BOTTOM: 6px;")
txtstream.WriteLine("    COLOR: white;")
txtstream.WriteLine("    PADDING-TOP: 6px;")
txtstream.WriteLine("    BORDER-BOTTOM: #999 1px solid;")
txtstream.WriteLine("    BACKGROUND-COLOR: navy;")
txtstream.WriteLine("    FONT-FAMILY: font-family: Cambria, serif;")
txtstream.WriteLine("    FONT-SIZE: 10px;")
txtstream.WriteLine("    text-align: left;")
txtstream.WriteLine("    white-Space: nowrap;")
txtstream.WriteLine("}")
txtstream.WriteLine("span")
txtstream.WriteLine("{")
txtstream.WriteLine("    BORDER-RIGHT: #999999 3px solid;")
txtstream.WriteLine("    PADDING-RIGHT: 3px;")
txtstream.WriteLine("    PADDING-LEFT: 3px;")
txtstream.WriteLine("    FONT-WEIGHT: Normal;")
txtstream.WriteLine("    PADDING-BOTTOM: 3px;")
txtstream.WriteLine("    COLOR: white;")
txtstream.WriteLine("    PADDING-TOP: 3px;")
txtstream.WriteLine("    BORDER-BOTTOM: #999 1px solid;")
txtstream.WriteLine("    BACKGROUND-COLOR: navy;")
txtstream.WriteLine("    FONT-FAMILY: font-family: Cambria, serif;")
txtstream.WriteLine("    FONT-SIZE: 10px;")
txtstream.WriteLine("    text-align: left;")
txtstream.WriteLine("    white-Space: nowrap;")
txtstream.WriteLine("    display:inline-block;")
```

txtstream.WriteLine("   width: 100%;")

txtstream.WriteLine("}")

txtstream.WriteLine("textarea")

txtstream.WriteLine("{")

txtstream.WriteLine("   BORDER-RIGHT: #999999 3px solid;")

txtstream.WriteLine("   PADDING-RIGHT: 3px;")

txtstream.WriteLine("   PADDING-LEFT: 3px;")

txtstream.WriteLine("   FONT-WEIGHT: Normal;")

txtstream.WriteLine("   PADDING-BOTTOM: 3px;")

txtstream.WriteLine("   COLOR: white;")

txtstream.WriteLine("   PADDING-TOP: 3px;")

txtstream.WriteLine("   BORDER-BOTTOM: #999 1px solid;")

txtstream.WriteLine("   BACKGROUND-COLOR: navy;")

txtstream.WriteLine("   FONT-FAMILY: font-family: Cambria, serif;")

txtstream.WriteLine("   FONT-SIZE: 10px;")

txtstream.WriteLine("   text-align: left;")

txtstream.WriteLine("   white-Space: nowrap;")

txtstream.WriteLine("   width: 100%;")

txtstream.WriteLine("}")

txtstream.WriteLine("select")

txtstream.WriteLine("{")

txtstream.WriteLine("   BORDER-RIGHT: #999999 3px solid;")

txtstream.WriteLine("   PADDING-RIGHT: 6px;")

txtstream.WriteLine("   PADDING-LEFT: 6px;")

txtstream.WriteLine("   FONT-WEIGHT: Normal;")

txtstream.WriteLine("   PADDING-BOTTOM: 6px;")

txtstream.WriteLine("   COLOR: white;")

txtstream.WriteLine("   PADDING-TOP: 6px;")

txtstream.WriteLine("   BORDER-BOTTOM: #999 1px solid;")

txtstream.WriteLine("   BACKGROUND-COLOR: navy;")

txtstream.WriteLine("   FONT-FAMILY: font-family: Cambria, serif;")

txtstream.WriteLine("   FONT-SIZE: 10px;")

txtstream.WriteLine("   text-align: left;")

```
txtstream.WriteLine("   white-Space: nowrap;")
txtstream.WriteLine("   width: 100%;")
txtstream.WriteLine("}")
txtstream.WriteLine("input")
txtstream.WriteLine("{")
txtstream.WriteLine("   BORDER-RIGHT: #999999 3px solid;")
txtstream.WriteLine("   PADDING-RIGHT: 3px;")
txtstream.WriteLine("   PADDING-LEFT: 3px;")
txtstream.WriteLine("   FONT-WEIGHT: Bold;")
txtstream.WriteLine("   PADDING-BOTTOM: 3px;")
txtstream.WriteLine("   COLOR: white;")
txtstream.WriteLine("   PADDING-TOP: 3px;")
txtstream.WriteLine("   BORDER-BOTTOM: #999 1px solid;")
txtstream.WriteLine("   BACKGROUND-COLOR: navy;")
txtstream.WriteLine("   FONT-FAMILY: font-family: Cambria, serif;")
txtstream.WriteLine("   FONT-SIZE: 12px;")
txtstream.WriteLine("   text-align: left;")
txtstream.WriteLine("   display:table-cell;")
txtstream.WriteLine("   white-Space: nowrap;")
txtstream.WriteLine("   width: 100%;")
txtstream.WriteLine("}")
txtstream.WriteLine("h1 {")
txtstream.WriteLine("color: antiquewhite;")
txtstream.WriteLine("text-shadow: 1px 1px 1px black;")
txtstream.WriteLine("padding: 3px;")
txtstream.WriteLine("text-align: center;")
txtstream.WriteLine("box-shadow: inset 2px 2px 5px rgba(0,0,0,0.5), inset -2px -2px 5px rgba(255,255,255,0.5)")
txtstream.WriteLine("}")
txtstream.WriteLine("</style>")
```

SHADOW BOX

```
txtstream.WriteLine("<style type='text/css>")
txtstream.WriteLine("body")
txtstream.WriteLine("{")
txtstream.WriteLine("    PADDING-RIGHT: 0px;")
txtstream.WriteLine("    PADDING-LEFT: 0px;")
txtstream.WriteLine("    PADDING-BOTTOM: 0px;")
txtstream.WriteLine("    MARGIN: 0px;")
txtstream.WriteLine("    COLOR: #333;")
txtstream.WriteLine("    PADDING-TOP: 0px;")
txtstream.WriteLine("    FONT-FAMILY: verdana, arial, helvetica, sans-serif;")
txtstream.WriteLine("}")
txtstream.WriteLine("table")
txtstream.WriteLine("{")
txtstream.WriteLine("    BORDER-RIGHT: #999999 1px solid;")
txtstream.WriteLine("    PADDING-RIGHT: 1px;")
txtstream.WriteLine("    PADDING-LEFT: 1px;")
txtstream.WriteLine("    PADDING-BOTTOM: 1px;")
txtstream.WriteLine("    LINE-HEIGHT: 8px;")
txtstream.WriteLine("    PADDING-TOP: 1px;")
txtstream.WriteLine("    BORDER-BOTTOM: #999 1px solid;")
txtstream.WriteLine("    BACKGROUND-COLOR: #eeeeee;")
txtstream.WriteLine("
filter:progid:DXImageTransform.Microsoft.Shadow(color='silver',      Direction=135,
Strength=16)")
txtstream.WriteLine("}")
txtstream.WriteLine("th")
txtstream.WriteLine("{")
txtstream.WriteLine("    BORDER-RIGHT: #999999 3px solid;")
txtstream.WriteLine("    PADDING-RIGHT: 6px;")
txtstream.WriteLine("    PADDING-LEFT: 6px;")
txtstream.WriteLine("    FONT-WEIGHT: Bold;")
txtstream.WriteLine("    FONT-SIZE: 14px;")
txtstream.WriteLine("    PADDING-BOTTOM: 6px;")
```

```
txtstream.WriteLine("    COLOR: darkred;")
txtstream.WriteLine("    LINE-HEIGHT: 14px;")
txtstream.WriteLine("    PADDING-TOP: 6px;")
txtstream.WriteLine("    BORDER-BOTTOM: #999 1px solid;")
txtstream.WriteLine("    BACKGROUND-COLOR: #eeeeee;")
txtstream.WriteLine("    FONT-FAMILY: font-family: Cambria, serif;")
txtstream.WriteLine("    FONT-SIZE: 12px;")
txtstream.WriteLine("    text-align: left;")
txtstream.WriteLine("    white-Space: nowrap;")
txtstream.WriteLine("}")
txtstream.WriteLine(".th")
txtstream.WriteLine("{")
txtstream.WriteLine("    BORDER-RIGHT: #999999 2px solid;")
txtstream.WriteLine("    PADDING-RIGHT: 6px;")
txtstream.WriteLine("    PADDING-LEFT: 6px;")
txtstream.WriteLine("    FONT-WEIGHT: Bold;")
txtstream.WriteLine("    PADDING-BOTTOM: 6px;")
txtstream.WriteLine("    COLOR: black;")
txtstream.WriteLine("    PADDING-TOP: 6px;")
txtstream.WriteLine("    BORDER-BOTTOM: #999 2px solid;")
txtstream.WriteLine("    BACKGROUND-COLOR: #eeeeee;")
txtstream.WriteLine("    FONT-FAMILY: font-family: Cambria, serif;")
txtstream.WriteLine("    FONT-SIZE: 10px;")
txtstream.WriteLine("    text-align: right;")
txtstream.WriteLine("    white-Space: nowrap;")
txtstream.WriteLine("}")
txtstream.WriteLine("td")
txtstream.WriteLine("{")
txtstream.WriteLine("    BORDER-RIGHT: #999999 3px solid;")
txtstream.WriteLine("    PADDING-RIGHT: 6px;")
txtstream.WriteLine("    PADDING-LEFT: 6px;")
txtstream.WriteLine("    FONT-WEIGHT: Normal;")
txtstream.WriteLine("    PADDING-BOTTOM: 6px;")
```

txtstream.WriteLine("   COLOR: navy;")

txtstream.WriteLine("   LINE-HEIGHT: 14px;")

txtstream.WriteLine("   PADDING-TOP: 6px;")

txtstream.WriteLine("   BORDER-BOTTOM: #999 1px solid;")

txtstream.WriteLine("   BACKGROUND-COLOR: #eeeeee;")

txtstream.WriteLine("   FONT-FAMILY: font-family: Cambria, serif;")

txtstream.WriteLine("   FONT-SIZE: 12px;")

txtstream.WriteLine("   text-align: left;")

txtstream.WriteLine("   white-Space: nowrap;")

txtstream.WriteLine("}")

txtstream.WriteLine("div")

txtstream.WriteLine("{")

txtstream.WriteLine("   BORDER-RIGHT: #999999 3px solid;")

txtstream.WriteLine("   PADDING-RIGHT: 6px;")

txtstream.WriteLine("   PADDING-LEFT: 6px;")

txtstream.WriteLine("   FONT-WEIGHT: Normal;")

txtstream.WriteLine("   PADDING-BOTTOM: 6px;")

txtstream.WriteLine("   COLOR: white;")

txtstream.WriteLine("   PADDING-TOP: 6px;")

txtstream.WriteLine("   BORDER-BOTTOM: #999 1px solid;")

txtstream.WriteLine("   BACKGROUND-COLOR: navy;")

txtstream.WriteLine("   FONT-FAMILY: font-family: Cambria, serif;")

txtstream.WriteLine("   FONT-SIZE: 10px;")

txtstream.WriteLine("   text-align: left;")

txtstream.WriteLine("   white-Space: nowrap;")

txtstream.WriteLine("}")

txtstream.WriteLine("span")

txtstream.WriteLine("{")

txtstream.WriteLine("   BORDER-RIGHT: #999999 3px solid;")

txtstream.WriteLine("   PADDING-RIGHT: 3px;")

txtstream.WriteLine("   PADDING-LEFT: 3px;")

txtstream.WriteLine("   FONT-WEIGHT: Normal;")

txtstream.WriteLine("   PADDING-BOTTOM: 3px;")

```
txtstream.WriteLine("    COLOR: white;")
txtstream.WriteLine("    PADDING-TOP: 3px;")
txtstream.WriteLine("    BORDER-BOTTOM: #999 1px solid;")
txtstream.WriteLine("    BACKGROUND-COLOR: navy;")
txtstream.WriteLine("    FONT-FAMILY: font-family: Cambria, serif;")
txtstream.WriteLine("    FONT-SIZE: 10px;")
txtstream.WriteLine("    text-align: left;")
txtstream.WriteLine("    white-Space: nowrap;")
txtstream.WriteLine("    display: inline-block;")
txtstream.WriteLine("    width: 100%;")
txtstream.WriteLine("}")
txtstream.WriteLine("textarea")
txtstream.WriteLine("{")
txtstream.WriteLine("    BORDER-RIGHT: #999999 3px solid;")
txtstream.WriteLine("    PADDING-RIGHT: 3px;")
txtstream.WriteLine("    PADDING-LEFT: 3px;")
txtstream.WriteLine("    FONT-WEIGHT: Normal;")
txtstream.WriteLine("    PADDING-BOTTOM: 3px;")
txtstream.WriteLine("    COLOR: white;")
txtstream.WriteLine("    PADDING-TOP: 3px;")
txtstream.WriteLine("    BORDER-BOTTOM: #999 1px solid;")
txtstream.WriteLine("    BACKGROUND-COLOR: navy;")
txtstream.WriteLine("    FONT-FAMILY: font-family: Cambria, serif;")
txtstream.WriteLine("    FONT-SIZE: 10px;")
txtstream.WriteLine("    text-align: left;")
txtstream.WriteLine("    white-Space: nowrap;")
txtstream.WriteLine("    width: 100%;")
txtstream.WriteLine("}")
txtstream.WriteLine("select")
txtstream.WriteLine("{")
txtstream.WriteLine("    BORDER-RIGHT: #999999 3px solid;")
txtstream.WriteLine("    PADDING-RIGHT: 6px;")
txtstream.WriteLine("    PADDING-LEFT: 6px;")
```

```
txtstream.WriteLine("    FONT-WEIGHT: Normal;")
txtstream.WriteLine("    PADDING-BOTTOM: 6px;")
txtstream.WriteLine("    COLOR: white;")
txtstream.WriteLine("    PADDING-TOP: 6px;")
txtstream.WriteLine("    BORDER-BOTTOM: #999 1px solid;")
txtstream.WriteLine("    BACKGROUND-COLOR: navy;")
txtstream.WriteLine("    FONT-FAMILY: font-family: Cambria, serif;")
txtstream.WriteLine("    FONT-SIZE: 10px;")
txtstream.WriteLine("    text-align: left;")
txtstream.WriteLine("    white-Space: nowrap;")
txtstream.WriteLine("    width: 100%;")
txtstream.WriteLine("}")
txtstream.WriteLine("input")
txtstream.WriteLine("{")
txtstream.WriteLine("    BORDER-RIGHT: #999999 3px solid;")
txtstream.WriteLine("    PADDING-RIGHT: 3px;")
txtstream.WriteLine("    PADDING-LEFT: 3px;")
txtstream.WriteLine("    FONT-WEIGHT: Bold;")
txtstream.WriteLine("    PADDING-BOTTOM: 3px;")
txtstream.WriteLine("    COLOR: white;")
txtstream.WriteLine("    PADDING-TOP: 3px;")
txtstream.WriteLine("    BORDER-BOTTOM: #999 1px solid;")
txtstream.WriteLine("    BACKGROUND-COLOR: navy;")
txtstream.WriteLine("    FONT-FAMILY: font-family: Cambria, serif;")
txtstream.WriteLine("    FONT-SIZE: 12px;")
txtstream.WriteLine("    text-align: left;")
txtstream.WriteLine("    display: table-cell;")
txtstream.WriteLine("    white-Space: nowrap;")
txtstream.WriteLine("    width: 100%;")
txtstream.WriteLine("}")
txtstream.WriteLine("h1 {")
txtstream.WriteLine("color: antiquewhite;")
txtstream.WriteLine("text-shadow: 1px 1px 1px black;")
```

```
txtstream.WriteLine("padding: 3px;")
txtstream.WriteLine("text-align: center;")
txtstream.WriteLine("box-shadow: inset 2px 2px 5px rgba(0,0,0,0.5), inset -
2px -2px 5px rgba(255,255,255,0.5)")
txtstream.WriteLine("}")
txtstream.WriteLine("</style>")
```

www.ingramcontent.com/pod-product-compliance
Lightning Source LLC
LaVergne TN
LVHW041216050326
832903LV00021B/645